The Tale of Ale-Hood

Original Text, Translations, and Word Lists

Translated by
Matthew Leigh Embleton

Copyright ©2025 Matthew Leigh Embleton. All rights reserved.

The Tale of Ale-Hood

The Tale of Ale-Hood (*Old Norse*) 4
Word List *(Old Norse to English)*..24
Word List *(English to Old Norse)* 36
The Tale of Ale-Hood (*Old Icelandic*)..46
Word List *(Old Icelandic to English)* 66
Word List *(English to Old Icelandic)*..78
A Word Comparison of Old Norse and Old Icelandic Words 88

Cover: Old Norse text over an outline of Iceland. Author's design.

The original Old Norse and Old Icelandic texts are in the public domain.
These translations ©2021 Matthew Leigh Embleton
©2025 Matthew Leigh Embleton (This Edition)

Acknowledgments

I have long been fascinated by languages and history, and I am very grateful to the special people in my life who have supported and encouraged me in my work. Thank you for believing in me. You know who you are.

Introduction

Old Norse is a North Germanic language spoken by inhabitants of Scandinavia from about the 7th to the 15th centuries. Old Icelandic is a variety of Old West Norse that emerged during the Norse settlement of Iceland in the second half of the 9th century. The rich tradition of Icelandic literature survived by oral tradition over several centuries before being written down in the 13th Century. The Tale of Ale-Hood (*Ölkofra þáttr*) is one of the many Tales of Icelanders or *Íslendingaþættir*. The word 'þáttr' (plural: '*þættir*') translates as a strand of rope or a yarn, comparable to the word 'yarn' in English sometimes used to refer to a story.

This book contains:
- The Tale of Ale-Hood (*Ölkofra þáttr*) (Old Norse Version)
- An Old Norse to English Word List
- An English to Old Norse Word List
- The Tale of Ale-Hood (*Ölkofra þáttr*) (Old Icelandic Version)
- An Old Icelandic to English Word List
- An English to Old Icelandic Word List
- A Word Comparison of Old Norse and Old Icelandic words

The texts are presented in their original form, with a literal word-for-word line-by-line translation, and a Modern English translation, all side-by-side. In this way, it is possible to see and feel how the worked and how it has evolved. This book is designed to be of use and interest to anyone with a passion for the Old Norse or Old Icelandic language, Norse history, or languages and history in general.

The Tale of Ale-Hood (Old Norse)

The Tale of Ale-Hood (*Old Norse*)

Old Norse	Literal	English
1	1	1
Þórhallr hét maðr.	Thorhall was-named a-man.	There was a man named Thorhall.
Hann bjó í Bláskógum á Þórhallsstöðum.	He lived in Blawoods in Thorhallsstead.	He lived in Blawoods in Thorhallsstead.
Hann var vel fjáreigandi ok heldr við aldr, er saga þessi gerðist.	He was well property-owning and rather with age, as story so happened.	He was a wealthy man and rather old when the story happened.
Litill var hann ok ljótr.	Small was he and ugly.	He was small and ugly.
Engi var hann íþróttamaðr; enn þó var hann hagr við járn ok tré.	None was he sports-man; but though was he handy with iron and wood.	He was not a sporty man but he was handy with iron and wood.
Hann hafði þá iðju, at gera öl á þingum, til fjár sér.	He had then occupation, to make ale at assembly, for wealth his.	He had a job making ale at the assembly to earn money
Enn af þeiri iðn varð hann brátt málkunnigr öllu stórmenni, því at þeir keyptu mest munngát.	And of their craft became he soon talking-known all great-men, because that they bought most ale.	and through this he came to talk to and get to know all the important people because they bought the most ale.
Var þá sem oft kann verða, at mungátin eru misjafnt vinsæl, ok svá þeir, er seldu.	Was then so often known was, that ale was uneven-in popularity, and so they, who sold.	As often happens, not everyone liked the ale, or the man who sold it.
Engi var Þórhallr veifiskati kallaðr ok heldr sjúkr.	None was Thorhall spendthrift called and rather stingy.	Thorhall was no spendthrift, and people said he was rather stingy.
Honum váru augu þung oftliga.	His were eyes heavy often.	His eyesight was poor.
Var þat siðr hans, at hafa kofra á höfði, ok jafnan á þingum.	Was it custom him, to have hood on head, and equally at assembly.	Often it was his habit to wear a hood, particularly at the assembly,

The Tale of Ale-Hood (Old Norse)

Old Norse	Literal	English
Enn af því at hann var maðr ekki nafnfrægr, þá gáfu þingmenn honum þat nafn, er við hann festist, at þeir kölluðu hann Ölkofra.	About of since that he was man not named, then gave assembly-men him the name, that with him fastened, that they called him Ale-Hood.	and since people could not remember his name, the assembly people nickhamed him Ale-Hood, and the name stuck.

2

Old Norse	Literal	English
Þat varð til tíðinda eitt haust, at Ölkofri fór í skóg þann, er hann átti, ok ætlaði at brenna kol, sem hann gerði.	It was to news one autumn, that Ale-Hood travelled to forest that, which he had, and intended to burn coal, which he made.	And so it was one autumn that Ale-Hood travelled to the woods where he intended to make charcoal.
Skógr sá var upp frá Hrafnabjörgum ok austr fyrir Lönguhlið.	Forest so was up from Hrafnabjorg and east from Langahlid.	The wood was north of Hrafnabjorg and east of Langahlid.
Hann dvaldist þar nökkura daga ok gerði til kola ok brendi síðan viðinn, ok vakti um nóttina yfir gröfunum.	He dwelled there some days and made to coal and burned since trees, and woke over night over pit.	He stayed there several days and made coal and then prepared the logs and kept watch over the pit.
Enn er á leið nóttina, þá sofnaði hann.	When was during the night, then slept he.	That was during the night, but then he fell asleep
Enn eldr kom upp í gröfunum ok hljóp í limit hjá, ok logaði þat brátt;	But fire came up in pit and ran to foliage beside, and blazed that soon;	and fire flared up in the pit and caught the branches and they were ablaze.
því næst hljóp eldr í skóginn;	then next ran fire to forest;	Then the fire ran through the next wood.
tók þá at brenna.	took then to burn.	It then began to burn.
Þá gerðist á vindr hvass.	Then was the wind sharp.	Then a sharp wind blew.
Nú vaknaði Ölkofri, ok varð því feginn, at hann gæti sér forðat.	Now awoke Ale-Hood, and was then relieved, that he got himself avoided.	Now Ale-Hood awoke and thought he was lucky to have avoided the fire.
Eldrinn hljóp í skóginn;	Fire ran among forest;	The fire ran through the woods.
brann þá skógr fyrst allr, er Ölkofri átti; enn síðan hljóp eldr í þá skóga, er þar váru næstir, ok brunnu skógar víða um hraunit.	burnt so forest first all, that Ale-Hood had; then afterwards ran fire to then forest, that there was nearest, and burned forests widely about lava-fields.	Burnt first were the woods that Ale-Hood owned, then the next woods, then afterwards the fire ran to the woods around the lava fields.

The Tale of Ale-Hood (Old Norse)

Old Norse	Literal	English
Er þar nú kallat á Svíðingi.	That there now called is Svidning.	There it is now called Svidning.
Þar brann skógr sá, er kallaðr var Goðaskógr.	There burned forest that, then called was Godaskogur.	There the wood was burned that was called Goda Wood.
Hann áttu sex goðar.	It had six chieftans.	It belonged to six chieftains.
Einn var Snorri goði, annarr Guðmundr Eyjólfsson, þriði Skafti lög-(sögu)maðr, fjórði Þórkell Geitisson, fimti Eyjólfr son Þórðar gellis, sétti Þórkell trefill Rauða-Bjarnarson.	One was Snorri chieftan, another Gudmund Son-of-Eyjolf, third Skafti law-speaker, fourth Thorkell Son-of-Geiti, fifth Eyjolf son Thord gellir, sixth Thorkell trefill Son-of-Rauda-Bjarn.	One chieftan was Snorri the Priest, another Gudmund Eyjolfson, Skafti the Lawspeaker, Thorkel Geitisson, Eyjolf son of Thord Gellir, and sixth Thorkell Trefill son of Red-Bear.
Þeir höfðu keypt skóga þessa, til þess at hafa til nytja sér á þingi.	They had bought forest then, to this to have to use themselves at assembly.	They had bought the wood for their own use at the assembly.
Eftir kolbrennu þessa reið Ölkofri heim.	After coal-burning this travelled Ale-Hood home.	After this coal burning Ale-Hood travelled home.
Tíðindi þessi spurðust víða um heruð, ok komu fyrst til Skafta þeira manna, er fyrir sköðum höfðu orðit.	News this asked many about district, and came first to Skafti of-the men, who for damage had word.	News about this was learned around the district and came to Skafti, the first of the six men whose woods had been damaged had word.
Um haustit sendi hann orð norðr til Eyjafjarðar með þeim mönnum, er ferð áttu milli heraða, ok lét segja Guðmundi skógabrennuna, ok þat með, at þat mál væri févænligt.	Around autumn sent he word north to Eyjafjord with those men, who travelled directions between districts, and let said Gudmund forest-burning, and with it, that the matter was money-promising.	Around autumn he sent word north to Eyafjord with men who travelled between districts and told Gudmund about the wood burning and with it that the matter could be profitable.
Slík sendiboð fóru ok vestr í heruð til þeira manna, er skóga höfðu átt.	Such sending-asked travelled and west to districts to those men, who forest had owned.	Such errands were travelled to the west, to the districts where the other owners were.
Fóru þá sendiboð um vetrinn eftir milli þeira allra, ok þat með, at goðar þessir sex skyldu hittast á þingi ok vera allir at einu ráði.	Travelled then messenger about winter after between they all, and to among, the chieftans these six should meet at assembly and be all as one counsel.	Messengers travelled through the winter between all six chieftains that they should meet at the assembly and take joint action

The Tale of Ale-Hood (Old Norse)

Old Norse	Literal	English
Enn Skafti skyldi mál til búa, því at hann sat næst.	As Skafti wished matter to settle, since that he sat nearest.	and Skafti would start the matter since he lived nearest.

3

Enn er vár kom, þá reið Skafti til með marga menn ok stefndi Ölkofra um skógabrennuna, ok lét varða skóggangssök.	In the spring came, then rode Skafti to with many men and summons Ale-Hood about forest-burning, and let concerning outlawry.	In the spring, at summons days, Skafti then rode with many men and summoned Ale-Hood for the burning of the wood under threat of outlawry.
Ölkofri var málóði ok heldr stórorðr; lét þess ván, ef vinir hans kœmi til þings, at Skafti mundi eigi jafnstórliga láta.	Ale-Hood was of-strong-language and rather high-sounding; let this wished, if friends his came to assembly, that Skafti would not equally-great leave.	Ale-Hood was swearing and shouting, and said that if his friends came to the assembly that Skafti would not be equally great.
Skafti svarar fá ok reið á brott.	Skafti answered few and rode to away.	Skafti answered little and rode away.
Um sumarit eftir komu þeir goðar sex til þings, er skógana höfðu átt, ok var þat ráðit, at mál skyldi frammi hafa, enn gera fé allmikit; ella hafa sjálfdæmi.	About summer after came chieftans they six to assembly, who forest owned had, and was it decided, the matter should from-forward have, as made fee all-much; otherwise have self-judgement.	In the summer the six chieftains who owned the woods came to the assembly and talked between themselves about the summons, and it was decided that the matter should be heavy damages if they could not have self-judgement.
Ölkofri kom til þings, ok átti munngát at selja.	Ale-Hood came to assembly, and had ale to sell.	Ale-Hood came to the assembly and had ale to sell,
Kom þá til fundar við vini sína, þá sem vanir váru at kaupa öl at honum.	Came then to meet with friends his, then as friends were to buy ale of him.	coming to meet with his friends who bought ale from him.
Hann bað þá liðs, ok bauð þeim öl at selja.	He invited then people, and offered them ale to sell.	He invited people and offered to sell them ale

The Tale of Ale-Hood (Old Norse)

Old Norse	Literal	English
Enn þeir svöruðu allir á einn veg, at þau ein kaup hefði þeir við átzt, at þeim var ekki vilnat í, — sögðu at þeir mundu eigi þeim birni beitast, at deila um mál hans við ofreflismenn slíka; ok vildi engi maðr heita honum liði, ok engi vildi eiga kaup við hann.	But they answered all the one way, that they only bought had they with affection, that they were not willed to, — said that they would not they bear employing, to share about the-matter his with ultra-strong-men such; and willed no man call him help, and none willed have buy with him.	but they all answered the same way, that they had not bought out of affection, and that they were not obliged to him, and they would not seek to get involved in his matter, especially since they were such powerful men, and no one wanted to help or even buy any of his ale.
Þótti honum þá heldr vandast málit.	Seemed to-him then rather difficult matter.	It looked to him that the situation was becoming rather tricky.
Gekk hann þá milli búða, ok fekk þó engi annsvör, þó at hann bæði menn liðs;	Went he then between booths, and got then no answers, though that he asked people help;	He then went among the booths and got no answers to his asking for help.
var þá lokit stórleika hans ok drambi.	Went he then between booths, and got then no answers, though that he asked people help;	He did not have any pride or arrogance left.
Þat var um dag einn, at Ölkofri kom til búðar Þórsteins Síðu-Hallssonar, ok gekk fyrir hann ok bað sér liðs.	That was about day one, that Ale-Hood came to booth Thorstein Son-of-Sidu-Hall, and got before him and asked his help.	It was one day that Ale-Hood came to the booth of Thorstein Hallsson and came before him and asked for his help.
Þórsteinn veitti honum slík annsvör sem aðrir.	Thorstein granted him such answer as others.	Thorstein gave him the same answer as the others.

4

Maðr er nefndr Broddi Bjarnason, mágr Þórsteins.	Man was named Broddi Bjarnason, brother-in-law Thorstein's.	There was a man camed Broddi Bjarnarson, Thorstein's brother-in-law.
Hann sat hit næsta honum.	He sat then next-to him.	He was sitting next to him.
Broddi var þá á tvítugs aldri.	Broddi was then about twenty aged.	Broddi was then aged about twenty.
Ölkofri gekk út með búðinni, þá er Þórsteinn hafði synjat honum liðs.	Ale-Hood went out-of among booths, then as Thorstein had refused him help.	Ale-Hood went out of the booth as Thorstein had refused to help him.

The Tale of Ale-Hood (Old Norse)

Old Norse	Literal	English
Broddi mælti þá:	Broddi said then:	Broddi then said:
"Svá lízt mér, mágr, sem þessi maðr sé ekki vel til skógarmanns feldr, ok er þat litilræði at sekja hann, þeim er miklir þykkjast menn fyrir sér.	"So like to-me, brother-in-law, that this man should not well to outlawry fall, and was it little-advised that seek him, they that great consider people therefore themselves.	"It seems to be brother-in-law that this man should not be an outlaw and it was mean-spirited that they seek this for him, those who consider themselves so important.
Nú er þér drengskapr, mágr, at veita þeim lið, er þíns liðs þarfnast".	Now is that word-of-honour, brother-in-law, that grant them help, that your assistance as-needed".	Now it would be honourable, brother-in-law, that we give him help and you appear as counsel".
Þórsteinn svarar:	Thorstein answered:	Thorstein answered:
"Veittú honum lið, ef þú ert allfúss til, enn veita mun ek þér gengi til þess sem annars".	"Grant him assistance, if you are all-happy to, and grant should i to-you going to this as others".	"Give him help if you are happy to, and I shall give you assistance on this path as I do others".
Broddi mælti þá við mann einn, at ganga skyldi eftir Ölkofra;	Broddi spoke then with man one, that go should after Ale-Hood;	Broddi spoke with a man and asked him to go after Ale-Hood.
sá gerði svá, — gekk út, ok þar hjá búðarveggnum hitti hann Ölkofra.	so done so, — went out, and there beside booth-walls found he Ale-Hood.	So it was done, he went out and there beside the booth walls he found Ale-Hood.
Stóð hann þar ok grét aumliga.	Stood he there and wept abjectly.	He was stood there weeping abjectly.
Þessi maðr bað hann ganga inn í búðina ok taka af sér ópit, "ok eigi skaltú snökta, er þú kemr til Þórsteins".	This man invited him to-go in to booth and take of him open, "and not shall-you sob, as you come to Thorstein".	The man invited him to go into the booth and stop himself shrieking "and don't be sobbing when you come to Thorstein".
Ölkofri varð grátfeginn ok gerði svá.	Ale-Hood became weeping-for-joy and did so.	Ale-Hood started weeping with joy and did so.
Enn er þeir komu fyrir Þórstein, þá tók Broddi til orða:	Then as they came before Thorstein, then took Broddi to words:	Then as they came before Thorstein then Broddi started to speak:
"Svá þykkir mér sem Þórsteinn vili þér lið veita, ok þykkir honum þetta klengisök vera;	"So seems to me Thorstein willing to-you assistance know, and seems to-him that small-blame be;	"So it seems to me Thorstein is willing to help you, and it seems to him that there is small blame.

The Tale of Ale-Hood (Old Norse)

Old Norse	Literal	English
máttir þú eigi gæta skóga þeira, er þú attir".	may you not guarded forest theirs, when you burned".	You may not have been able to guard against their woods burning when your own had burned down.
Ölkofri mælti:	Ale-Hood said:	Ale-Hood said:
"Hverr er sjá hinn sæli maðr, er nú mælir við mik?"	"Who is this the good man, that now speaks with me?"	"Who is this good man that now speaks with me?"
"Broddi heiti ek", segir hann.	"Broddi named i", said he.	"I am named Broddi", he said.
Þá mælti Ölkofri:	Then spoke Ale-Hood:	Then Ale-Hood spoke:
"Hvárt er hér Broddi Bjarnason?"	"Which is here Broddi Bjarnason?"	"He who is named Broddi Bjarnarson?"
"Svá er", segir Broddi.	"So is", said Broddi.	"So it is", said Broddi.
"Bæði er", kvað Ölkofri, "at þú ert göfigligri at sjá enn aðrir menn, enda áttu til þess varit".	"Both are", said Ale-Hood, "that you are nobler to this than other people, in-the-end have to this defend".	"Both are", said Ale-Hood, "that you are nobler to see than other men, in-the-end to your family's worth",
Fór hann þar mörgum orðum um, ok gerist þá hraustr í máli.	For he there many words about, and was then brave to speak.	and he went on to speak many words about it and became braver.
"Hitt er nú til", kvað Þórsteinn, "ef þú ert allfúss til, Broddi, at veita honum nökkut lið, er þó lofar hann þik svá mjök".	"Find i now to", said Thorstein, "if you are all-happy to, Broddi, to grant him some assistance, as though praises he you so much".	"Now I find towards", said Thorstein, "if you are happy to give him some assistance since he praises you so much".
Broddi stóð þá upp ok margt manna með honum.	Broddi stood then up and many men with him.	Broddi then stood up, and with many many with him.
Gekk hann út ór búðinni.	Went he from out-of booth.	He went out of his booth.
Hafði Broddi þá Ölkofra á einmæli ok ræddi við hann.	He Drew then Ale-Hood to one-talk and discussed with him.	He then took Ale-Hood to talk privately and discuss with him.
Síðan ganga þeir upp á völluna;	Afterwards went they up to plains;	Afterwards they went up to the assembly plains.
var þar fyrir margt manna.	were there before many men.	There were many men before them.

The Tale of Ale-Hood (Old Norse)

Old Norse	Literal	English
Höfðu þeir þá verit í lögréttu.	Had they then been at law-assembly.	They had been at the law-assembly.

5

Old Norse	Literal	English
Enn er aðrir menn höfðu í brott gengit, þá sátu þeir eftir Guðmundr ok Skafti, ok rœddu um lög.	And as other men had to away walked, then sat they behind Gudmund and Skafti, and discussed about law.	As the other men left, there sat behind Gudmund and Skafti discussing law.
Broddi ok förunautar hans reikuðu um völluna, enn Ölkofri gekk í lögréttuna.	Broddi and companions his roamed about plains, but Ale-Hood went to law-assembly.	Broddi and his companions walked about the assembly plains but Ale-Hood went to the law-assembly.
Hann fell til jarðar allr, ok kraup til fóta þeim ok mælti:	He fell to earth all, and kneeled about feet them and said:	He fell to the ground and kneeled at their feet among them and said:
"Sæll er ek orðinn, er ek hefi ykkr fundit, hina dýrligu menn ok höfðingja mína, eðr munu þit nökkut vilja mér hjálpa, hinir góðu menn, þótt ek sé ómakligr; því at ek verð nú allr fyrir borði, nema þit dugit mér".	"Happy am i become, that i have you found, then dearly men and chieftans mine, but shall you some wish to-me help, other good men, though i so uncomfortable; because that i deserve not all before borne, take you enough of-me".	"I am happy to have found you my dear men and chieftains, but should some of you wish to help me, good people, though I do not deserve it, I am uncomfortable because now I will be all before the table unless enough of you are with me?"
Seint er at telja öll orð Ölkofra, þau er hann mælti, ok lét hann sem aumligast á allan hátt.	Late is to tell all words Ale-hood's, his that he spoke, and let him as miserable in every way.	It would take too long to tell all of Ale-Hood's words that he spoke as he was miserable in every way.
Þá mælti Guðmundr til Skafta:	Then said Gudmund to Skafti:	Then Gudmund said to Skafti:
"Allvesalliga lætr þessi maðr".	"Miserable behaviour this man".	"What miserable behaviour from this man".
Skafti svarar:	Skafti answered:	Skafti answered:

The Tale of Ale-Hood (Old Norse)

Old Norse	Literal	English
"Hvar er nú, Ölkofri, stórlæti þitt? Ólíkligt þótti mér í vár, þá er vér fórum stefnuför, at sá mundi þinn hinn bezti kostr, at leggja málit undir mik; eðr hversu drjúgir verða þeir þér nú í liðveizlunni, höfðingjarnir, er þú hœttir mér í vár?"	"Where is now, Ale-Hood, pride yours Unlike seem you as spring, then as we travelled summons, to-you so could you the best choice, to allow the-matter under me; but how substantial were they to-you now the supportive, chieftans, that you mannered to-me about spring?"	"Where is your pride now Ale-Hood? You seem different from the spring when we travelled to summon you, so you could make the best choice to have the matter judged by me, but how substantial have you found the supportive chieftains that you threatened me with in the spring?"
Ölkofri svarar:	Ale-Hood said:	Ale-Hood said:
"Œrr var ek þá, ok þó verr, er ek vilda þat eigi, at þú dœmdir um mitt mál, enda gettú eigi höfðingja, því at þeir eru órhjarta allir, þegar þeir sjá ykkr at koma.	"Awed was i then, and though worse, am i willed it not, to you deem about my matter, in-the-end getting no chieftans, because that they were un-heartened all, as-soon-as they saw you that came.	"I was awed then, and worse that I willed it not to be judged by you in the matter, getting no chieftains in the end because they were disheartened as soon as they saw that you had come.
Sæll væra ek þá, ef ek næða því, at koma undir ykkr mínu máli.	Happy would-be i then, if i neared therefore, to come under you my matter.	How happy I would be if I could be nearer to my matter coming under you.
Eigi á ek nökkura ván þess, enn várkunn er þér, Skafti minn, at þú hafir mér svá reiðst, at nú sé þess engi kostr.	But to i some hope this, then pity i that, Skafti mine, that you have to-me such counsel, that now see this none choice.	But what hope is there of this? Then it is a pity that you have given me such counsel that I now see this is not a choice.
Var ek þá fól ok afglapi, er ek neitaða gerð þinni.	Was i then fool and simpleton, that i refusal made yours.	I was then a fool and a simpleton to refuse your offer
Enn ek þori eigi at sjá þá grimmu menn, er þegar munu drepa mik, ef þit hjálpit mér eigi við".	That i greater-part not to saw then grim men, that straight-away will kill me, if you help me not with".	that I saw no greater part then, the terrible men that will kill me straight away if you do not help me with this".
Hann mælti oft hit sama; sagði ok at hann þóttist sæll, ef þeir skyldi dœma hans mál.	He spoke often the same; said and that he thought happy, if they should deem his matter.	He often said the same things, saying that he thought he would be happy if they should judge the matter.
"Þykki mér þar mitt fé bezt komit, er þit hafit".	"Think i that my money best comes, that you have".	"I think that my money would be best if you have it".
Guðmundr mælti til Skafta:	Gudmund said to Skafti:	Gudmund spoke to Skafti:

The Tale of Ale-Hood (Old Norse)

Old Norse	Literal	English
"Ekki ætla ek þenna vel til sektar fallinn, eðr mun eigi hitt heldr ráð, at vér gerim hann feginn, ok látim hann kjósa menn til gerðar þessar.	"Not intend i that well to guilt fall, but should not find rather advice, to we being he relieved, and let he choose people to do this.	"I don't suppose it will be well if he falls guilty, and should it not rather be the decision left with him to choose people to do this? Though I know not how others alike is this matter agreed with him".
Þó veit ek eigi, hversu hinum líkar, er eigu þetta mál við hann".	Though know i not, how-so others alike, is said-of this matter with him".	Though I don't know how others are alike in this matter being agreed with him".
"Nú þá, hinir góðu menn", segir Ölkofri, "veitit mér þá nökkurn dugnað eftir".	"Now then, other good men", said Ale-Hood, "know i then someone assistance after".	"Now then other good men", said Ale-Hood, "I know then that you will give me some assistance after".
Skafti mælti:	Skafti said:	Skafti said:
"Undir mér er lykt máls þessa, því at ek fer með sökina.	"Under me is conclusion matter this, therefore that i go with seeking.	"Under me is the judgement of this matter, therefore I will seek to resolve it.
Munum vér til þess hætta, Ölkofri, at vit Guðmundr gerim um ok lúkim málinu.	Should on to this end, Ale-Hood, that with Gudmund be about and conclude case.	So to that end, Ale-Hood, the case will be concluded with Gudmund.
Get ek, at þér muni þat duga við fullting okkart".	Get i, that you would that help with assistance ours".	That is how it would help you with our assistance".

6

Þá stóð Ölkofri upp, ok takast þeir síðan í hendr.	Then stood Ale-Hood up, and took them then in hand.	Then Ale-Hood stood up and took them then in hand.
Nefndi Ölkofri þegar vátta, hveru at öðrum, ok er váttnefna kom upp, þá drifu menn at.	Named Ale-Hood then witness, each to others, and as witnesses came up, then flocked many to.	Ale-Hood then named each of his witnesses, and many people crowded around.
Nefndi Ölkofri fyrst Brodda ok föruneyti hans.	Named Ale-Hood first Brodda and companions his.	Ale-Hood named Broddi and his companions.
Skafti mælti:	Skafti spoke:	Skafti spoke:

The Tale of Ale-Hood (Old Norse)

Old Norse	Literal	English
"Sökunautr várr biðr okkr Guðmund til gerðar um mál þetta, enn þó at vit hafim þat staðfest með oss, er skaða höfum fengit, at sjálfdœmi skyldi fyrir koma, þá viljum vit Guðmundr þat nú veita honum, at vit gerim heldr um enn aðrir, ef Þórhallr vill þat kjörit hafa.	"Defendant our invited us Gudmund to do about matter this, and though that we have that confirmed with us, that damages have got, to self-judgement should by coming, then will we Gudmund that now provide him, to with doing rather of the others, if Thorhall wishes that choice have.	"The defendant has invited Gudmund and myself to do about this matter, and though we have confirmed that those who suffered the loss are to accept self-judgement, Gudmund and I are willing to grant Ale-Hood this much, that we two rather than any other men shall decide the matter if Thorhall agrees.
Skulu þér þess nefndir váttar, at fyrir mál þetta skal fé gera enn eigi mannsektir.	Should you this name witnesses, as for the-matter that shall money make about only fines.	You should stand witness for the matter that only damages shall be awarded.
Ek handsala niðrfall at sökum þeim, er ek stefnda í vár".	I confirm dropping the blame those, that i summonsed in spring".	I confirm that I drop the charge for which I summoned him in the spring.
Síðan slitu þeir handlaginu.	After dissolved they handshake.	Then they dissolved with a handshake.
Þá mælti Skafti við Guðmund:	Then spoke Skafti with Gudmund:	Then Skafti spoke with Gudmund.
"Því mun eigi vel, at vit lúkim þessu af?"	"Why should not well, that we conclude this of?"	"Why don't we conclude this?"
"Vel má þat", segir Guðmundr.	"Well may that", said Gudmund.	"That may well be", said Gudmund.
Ölkofri mælti:	Ale-Hood spoke:	Ale-Hood spoke:
"Ekki skulu þit hrapa því svá, því at er ekki ráðinn í, at kjósa ykkr, heldr enn aðra menn".	"Not should you hurry therefore so, for that am not decided of, to choose you, rather than other people".	"You should not be in such a hurry, because I have not decided if I choose you or rather someone else".
Guðmundr mælti:	Gudmund spoke:	Gudmund spoke:
"Svá var skilt, at vér skyldim gera, nema þú kjörir heldr þá aðra, er þetta mál eigu með okkr".	"So was divided, that we should do, taking your choice rather then others, that this matter have with us".	"It was so agreed that Skafti and I would decide rather than others who would have this matter with us".
Ölkofri mælti:	Ale-Hood said:	Ale-Hood said:

14

The Tale of Ale-Hood (Old Norse)

Old Norse	Literal	English
"Því neitaða ek alla tíma, at þeir skyldi gera; enn svá var skilit í handlaginu, at ek skylda kjósa tvá menn til, þá er ek vilda".	"Since refused i all time, that they should do; about so was divided at agreement, that i should choose two men for, then as i willed".	"I never agreed at the time that these men should decide, it was agreed at the handshake that I could choose any two men I wanted".
Þá var leitat um handsals-vætti.	Then was sought about agreement.	Then the agreement was sought about the assembly,
Enn þingmenn Guðmundar ok Skafta deildust allmjök at, hversu skilit var; enn Broddi ok förunautar hans skáru skýrt ór, at svá hefði skilit verit sem Ölkofri sagði, at hann skyldi kjósa menn til gerðar.	The assembly Gudmund and Skafta judged all-greatly that, how understood was; that Broddi and companions his cut clear of, that so had understood been which Ale-Hood said, that he should choose man to do.	Gudmund and Skafti disagreed greatly about how it had been agreed, but Broddi and his companions were clear about how it was understood, as Ale-Hood had said, that he could choose the men to decide.
Þá mælti Skafti:	Then spoke Skafti:	Then Skafti Spoke:
"Hvaðan rann sjá alda undir? Ok sé ek, at þú heldr nökkuru rakkara halanum, enn fyrir stundu áðan.	"Where runs this wave from-beneath And see i, that you rather somewhat bolder tail-wagging, than before awhile earlier.	"Where runs this wave from beneath you Ale-Hood? I see that you are wagging your tail more boldy than before,
Eðr hverja menn muntú kjósa til gerðar?"	But what men should choose to do?"	and which men do you choose to decide?
Ölkofri mælti:	Ale-Hood spoke:	Ale-Hood spoke:
"Ekki skal lengi at því hyggja.	"Not shall longer to for think.	"I shall think on it no longer.
Ek kýs Þórstein Hallsson ok Brodda Bjarnason mág hans, ok ætla ek, at þá sé málit betr komit, enn þit gerit um".	I choose Thorstein Hallsson and Brodda Bjarnason brother-in-law his, and intend i, that then so matter better comes, than you make about".	I choose Thorstein Hallsson and his brother-in-law Broddi Bjarnarson, and I suppose that the matter will be better than if undertaken by you".
Skafti sagði, at hann ætlaði, at þat mál væri vel komit, þótt þeir gerði um,	Skafti said, to him intended, that this matter would-be well coming, though they made about,	Skafti said to him that he supposed that this matter would be in good hands if they undertook it.
því at málaefni vár eru brýn ok góð; enn þeir eru svá vitrir, at þeir munu sjá kunna, hversu þungs þú ert af verðr.	as the matters are they urgent and good; and they are so wise, that they should this know, how-so heavily you are of worth.	"As the case is urgent and just and they are wise men, they should know how heavily you shall be dealt with".

The Tale of Ale-Hood (Old Norse)

Old Norse	Literal	English
Ölkofri gekk þá í lið Brodda, ok fóru menn heim til búða.	Ale-Hood went then with company Brodda's, and travelled men home to booths.	Ale-Hood went then with Brodda's company and the men travelled home to their booths.

7

Old Norse	Literal	English
Eftir um daginn skyldi upp segja sætt.	Later in the-day should up said settlement.	Later in the day the verdict was to be announced.
Báru þeir þá ráð sín saman Þórsteinn ok Broddi.	Bore they then matter theirs together Thorstein and Broddi.	Thorstein and Broddi started to consider the matter.
Vildi Þórsteinn meira gera; enn Broddi kvað þat skýrst, at gera svá sem hann vildi, ok segja þá sjálfr sátt upp.	Willed Thorstein more to-do; than Broddi said it clarified, to be so as he willed, and say then himself settlement up.	Thorstein wanted more of a settlement than Broddi did, and it was agreed that it would be as he said.
Broddi bað hann kjósa, hvárt er hann vildi:	Broddi asked him choose, either as he willed:	Broddi invited him to choose either as he wished,
segja sjálfr sátt upp, eðr sitja fyrir svörum, ef nökkurir menn yrði til, at leita á gerðina.	say yourself settlement up, or sit before answers, if some men be to, the objection to make.	to decide the settlement or sit in judgement and answer any objections.
Þórsteinn lézt heldr vilja segja sátt upp, enn skifta hnœfilyrðum við þá goðana.	Thorstein let rather willed say settlement up, than exchange blows with then chieftans.	Thorstein said that he would rather give the judgement than exchange blows with the chieftains.
Síðan sagði Þórsteinn, at Ölkofri skyldi eigi lengi þurfa síns hluta at bíða; kvað þá skyldu gjaldast féit allt at Lögbergi.	Since said Thorstein, that Ale-Hood should not long need his lot to wait; said then should pay fee altogether at Law-Rock.	Then Thorstein said that Ale-Hood would not need to wait long, saying that then the payment of a fee should be made altogether at the law rock.
Síðan gengu þeir til Lögbergs.	Then went they to Law-Rock.	Then they went to the law rock.
Enn er lokit var þar lögskil at mæla, þá spurði Þórsteinn Hallsson, hvárt goðar þeir væri at Lögbergi, er mál áttu at kæra við Ölkofra.	And when ended were there legal-settlement to matters, then asked Thorstein Hallsson, whether chieftans they were at Law-Rock, that matter had to accuse with Ale-Hood.	And when the other legal settlements were done, Thorstein Halsson asked whether the chieftains who had brought the accusation against Ale-Hood were present:
"Mér er svá sagt, at vit Broddi skylim gera um mál þat.	"To-me is so said, that with Broddi should make about matter that.	"It has been said to me that Broddi and I shall settle the matter.

The Tale of Ale-Hood (Old Norse)

Old Norse	Literal	English
Munum vit nú upp lúka gerðinni, ef þér vilit til hlýða".	Should with now up finish make, if you will to listen".	We shall deliver the conclusion if you are ready to listen".
Þeir sögðust góðs at vænta, er þeir mundu ráttlátir í gerðinni.	They said good to expect, that they would right-like to make.	They said they expected the decision would be just.
Þá mælti Þórsteinn:	Then spoke Thorstein:	Then Thorstein spoke:
"Svá lízt okkr á, sem lítils sé fyrir vert um skóga yðra félaga;	"So beholding ours is, that little being for worth about forest yours companions;	"So is our finding that your wood and that of your companions is of little worth.
váru þeir félitlir ok fjarlægir yðr til gagns.	were they fee-little and financial yours little benefit.	They were worth very little financially for you to benefit.
Var eigingirni í mikil þeira manna, er góðs áttu kost, ok kalla þat með eign sinni annarri.	Was selfish that much these men, the chieftans had benefit, and call that with may opinion another.	It was a great selfishness that these chieftains had benefitted from this property in this way,
Enn hann mátti eigi ábyrgjast yðvarn skóg, er hann brendi sinn skóg, ok eru slíkt váðaverk.	That he may not guarantee your forest, that he burned his forest, and are such accidents.	and another opinion is that he could not have guaranteed to save your woods once his had burned, and it is therefore as such an accident.
Enn fyrir því, at þat er í gerð lagt, þá skal gera nökkut fyrir.	But for because, that it is to made laid, then shall be-done something for.	But because this settlement is to be made then something shall be done.
Þér sex menn hafit átt skógana.	Then six men have had forests.	These six men who own the woods.
Nú viljum vit gera sex álnir hverjum yðrum, ok skal þat gjaldast hér þegar".	Now will we make six measures each yours, and shall that be-paid here straightaway".	Now we will award six measures, one for each of you that shall be paid here immediately".
Broddi hafði við búizt, ok stikat vaðmál í sundr, ok kastar hann sérhverjum stúf til þeira ok mælti:	Broddi had with prepared, and stitched homespun-cloth to asunder, and cast he theirs stump to them and said:	Broddi had prepared and stitched a homespun cloth and cast each strip down to them and said:
"Slikt kalla ek arga skatt".	"Such call i a-dog's tax".	I call this a tribute to the dastardly.
Skafti svarar:	Skafti said:	Skafti said:

The Tale of Ale-Hood (Old Norse)

Old Norse	Literal	English
"Auðsætt er þat, Broddi, at þú ert fúss til at eiga illt við oss.	"Obvious is it, Broddi, that you are willing to that have ill with us.	"It is obvious Broddi that you wish to have bad will with us.
Hefir þú mjök stungizt til þessa máls, ok ferr þú lítt þverr á fœti at fjandskap við oss;	Have you much wounded about this matter, and go you little around on foot to fiend-ship with us;	You have made a great wound in this matter, and you do not tip-toe around making enemies of us.
kann vera at oss falli önnur mál léttra".	can be that ours fall another matter easier".	It can be that other law suits will be resolved more easily".
Broddi svarar:	Broddi answered:	Broddi answered:
"Þurfu muntú þess Skafti, at taka meira á öðrum sakferlum, ef skerða skal í þat skarð, er Ormr frændi þinn reytti af þér, fyrir mansöngsdrápu, er þú ortir um konu hans.	"Need should this Skafti, to take more of other lawsuits, if action shall to that gap, that Orm kinsmen yours tried of you, for love-song-poem, that you worded about wife his.	You need to make more money from other law suits, Skafti, to make up for the damages your kinsman Orm got from you for the love-poem you composed about his wife.
Var þat illa gert, enda var þat illa goldit".	Was that ill done, in-the-end was that ill paid".	Was that bad will all paid in the end?"
Þá mælti Þórkell trefill:	Then spoke Thorkell trefill:	Then Thorkell Trefill spoke:
"Allmjök missýnist slíkum manni sem Broddi er;	"All-much mistake such man as Broddi that;	"That was very much a mistake from such a man as Broddi.
hann vill hafa vináttu Ölkofra, eðr nökkurar mútugjafir, ok kaupa svá, at gera sér at óvinum slíka menn, sem hann hefir í fangi".	he will have friendship Ale-hood's, or some bribes, and bought so, that made his to un-friends such men, as he has to enemies".	That he will have Ale-Hood's friendship, or his bribes, so that he makes his opponents into enemies".
Broddi svarar:	Broddi said:	Broddi said:
"Ekki er þat missýni, at halda einurð sinni, þótt mannamunr sé með yðr Ölkofra;	"Not is that mistake, to hold determined his, thought integrity as with yours Ale-Hood;	"It is no mistake to hold with determination to your integrity, yours or Ale-Hood's.

The Tale of Ale-Hood (Old Norse)

Old Norse	Literal	English
enn hitt var glámsýni í vár, er þú reitt til várþings, at þú varaðist eigi þat, er Steingrimr hafði stóðhest selfeitan, ek lagðist hann upp at baki þér; enn merin sú, er þú reitt var mögr, ok fell hún undir þér ok hefi ek eigi spurt til sanns, hverjum þá slöðraði; enn hitt sá menn, at þú vart lengi fastr, því at hestrinn lagði fœtrna fram yfir kápuna".	but find then big-mistake in spring, when you rode to local-assembly, that you warned not-of it, that Steingrim had stallion fat, and laid he up to back you; as mare yours, were you riding was skinny, and fell she under you also have i not asked about the-truth, whether then trailing-behind; about found this people, that you were long fastened, with the horse laid feet from across cloak".	But you yourself made a big mistake in the spring when you rode to a local assembly, you were not aware of the fat stallion that Steingrim had until he was laid up to your backside, and you were riding that skinny mare as she fell under you, and I have never learned the truth whether those trailing behind you found that you were long fastened with the horse with his feet laid across your cloak".
Eyjólfr Þórðarson mælti:	Eyjolf Thordarson spoke:	Eyjolf Thordarson spoke:
"Þat er satt at segja, at sjá maðr hefir allmjök dregit bust ór nefi oss, enda mælir rán ok regin við oss á svá gert ofan".	"It is true to say, that this man has all-much drawn cheated from noses ours, in-the-end talking robbery and ruling with us by saying done over".	"It is true that this man has cheated us out of our reward in front of our noses, and heaping abuse over us".
Broddi svarar:	Broddi said:	Broddi said:
"Eigi hefi ek dregit bust ór nefi yðr.	"Not have i drawn cheated of noses yours.	"I have not cheated you of your noses.
Þá var dregin bust ór nefi þér, er þú fórt norðr til Skagafjarðar ok stalt öxnum frá Þórkeli Eirekssyni; enn Goðdala-Starri reið eftir þér, ok sáttu þá eftirförina, er þér varut komnir í Vatnsdal.	Then were drawn cheated of nose you, as you travelled north to Skagafjord and stealing oxen from Thorkell Eriksson; and Guddala-Starri rode after you, and saw-you then after-travelling, that you were coming to Vatnsdal.	You were cheated of your nose as you travelled north to Skagafjord stealing oxen from Thorkell Eriksson and Guddala-Starri rode after you, and then you reached Vatnsdal.
Varðtú þá svá hræddr, at þú brátt þér í merarlíki, ok váru slíkt firn mikil; enn þeir Starri ráku aftr öxnina, ok var þat satt, at hér dró bust ór nefi þér".	Were-you then so scared, that you transformed you to mare-like, and were so awful much; that they Starri drove back oxen, and was that true, that he drew cheated of nose you".	You were so scared that you turned yourself into a mare, an awful thing to do, and Starri drove the oxen back, so it is true, he cheated your nose".
Þá mælti Snorri goði:	Then spoke Snorri chieftan:	Then Snorri the chieftain spoke:

The Tale of Ale-Hood (Old Norse)

Old Norse	Literal	English
"Allt er oss annat tiltœkilegt, enn deila hér illyrðum við Brodda; enn þat er líkast, at vér gerim oss minnisamt um fjandskap þenna, er Broddi lýsír við oss, ef vér komumst í fœri".	"All are we other available, than sharing here malice with Broddi; but it is likely, that we make us memorable about fiend-ship this, that Broddi declared with us, if we come to opportunity".	We would all rather be unavailable than here sharing malice with Broddi, but it is likely that we shall have it remembered what fiendship Broddi has shown us, and how it has come to be.
Broddi svarar:	Broddi said:	Broddi said:
"Um snýr þú þá sœmdunum, Snorri, ef þú leggr allan hug á at hefna mér, enn þú hefnir eigi föður þíns".	"Around turned you then honour, Snorri, if you lay all mind to that revenge to-me, than you avenge not father yours".	"Your honour is turned around then, Snorri, if you put your mind to revenge that instead of avenging your father".
Þá mælti Þórkell Geitisson:	Then spoke Thorkell Geitisson:	Then Thorkell Geitisson spoke:
"Þetta er líkast, at þú hafir þat helzt af nafni því, er þú ert eftir heitinn, at hann vildi hvers manns hlut óhœfan af sér verða láta, ok þat annat at menn þoli eigi, ok liggir þú drepinn, er stundir líða".	"It is likely, that you have that held of the-name of, that you are after named, that he wills each man's lot trouble of himself being let, and that other of men tolerate not, and laying you killed, be awhile passed".	It is likely, that all you have held of the name your father gave to you, is to make trouble with every man, other men will not tolerate it and you may be killed after a while.
Broddi svarar:	Broddi said:	Broddi said:
"Engi vegr er okkr i, frændi, at yppa hér fyrir alþýðu ógæfu frænda várra; enn ekki skal þat dylja, er margir vitu, at Brodd-Helgi var veginn.	"No way is ours of, kinsmen, that up here before the-people un-giving kinsmen talking-loudly; about not shall this disguise, that many knowing, that Brodd-Helgi was killed.	"There is no way to gain anything, kinsmen, by talking loudly, this shall not disguise that many know that Brodd-Helgi was killed.
Var mér ok þat sagt, at faðir þinn tœki ofarliga til þeira launanna; enn hitt ætla ek, ef þú leitar at, at þú munir fingrum kenna þat, er faðir minn markaði þik í Böðvarsdal".	Was i and that told, that father yours took high-up to their loans; but find suppose i, if you seek that, as you should fingers know that, was father mine marked you in Bodvarsdale".	I was told that your father paid the highest price, but I suppose that if you find your fingers, then they will find where my father marked you at Bodvarsdale".
Eftir þat skildust þeir, ok gengu heim til búða.	After that separated they, and none home to booths.	After that they separated and went back home to their booths.
Er nú Ölkofri ór sögunni.	Is now Ale-Hood out-of the-saga.	Ale-Hood is now out of the saga.

The Tale of Ale-Hood (Old Norse)

Old Norse	Literal	English
8	**8**	**8**
Annan dag eftir gekk Broddi til búðar Þorkels Geitissonar ok inn í búðina, ok kastaði orðum á Þórkel.	Next day after went Broddi to booth Thorkell Geitisson's and in to booth, and cast words to Thorkell.	The next day afterwards Broddi went to Thorkell Geitisson's booth and exchanged words with Thorkell.
Hann svarar fá, ok var hinn reiðasti.	He answered few, and was the most-angry.	He answered little and was very angry.
Broddi mælti:	Broddi spoke:	Broddi spoke:
"Því er ek hér kominn, frændi, at ek sá missmíði á því, er ek talaða við þik.	"For am i here coming, kinsman, that i saw mistake in what, was i said with you.	"For I have come here, kinsman, because I saw a mistake in what I said to you.
Vil ek þess biðja, at þú virðir mér þat til berusku ok óvizku, en látum eigi frændsemi okkra at verri.	Will i this ask, that you value me that to childishness and unwise, but let-us not kinship ours to worsen.	I wish to ask you, though you find me given to childishness, and unwise, let our kinship not worsen.
Er hér sverð búit, er ek vil gefa þér;	Is here sword to-settle, that i will give to-you;	Here is a sword that I will give to you to settle.
vil ek, at þat fylgi, at þá farir at heimboði til mín í sumar, ok skal því lýsa, at eigi skulu betri gripir í minni eigu enn þeir, er þú skalt þiggja".	will i, to this follow, that you travel to home-booth to mine in summer, and shall that show, that none shall better treasures of mine own than this, that you shall receive".	I would like to follow this by inviting you to travel to my home booth in summer, and I will show you that I have no treasures finer than the ones that you shall receive here".
Þórkell tók þessu þakksamliga; sagði, at hann var þess fúss, at þeir gerði góða sína frændsemi.	Thorkell took these thankfully; said, that he was this willing, that they made good their kinship.	Thorkell took this gladly, and said that he was willing to make good their kinship.
Gekk þá Broddi heim.	Went then Broddi home.	Broddi then went home.
Þat var aftaninn fyrir þinglausnir, at Broddi gekk vestr yfir á; enn við brúarsporðinn hittust þeir Guðmundr, ok varð ekki at kveðjum.	That was back for assembly-ending, that Broddi went west over river; and with footbridge found they Gudmund, and were not to greet.	It was the last day of the assembly that Broddi went west over the river, and at a footbridge he met Gudmund, and neither greeted the other.
Ok er þeir skildust, þá veik Guðmundr aftr ok mælti:	And as they separated, then gave Gudmund back and said:	And as they passed each other Gudmund looked back and said:

The Tale of Ale-Hood (Old Norse)

Old Norse	Literal	English
"Hverja leið skaltu riða af þingi, Broddi?" Hann sneri aftr ok mælti:	"What way shall-you ride from assembly, Broddi?" He turned back and said:	Which way will you ride back from the Assembly, Broddi?
"Ef þér er forvitni á því, þá mun ek riða um Kjöl til Skagafjarðar; þá til Eyjafjarðar, þaðan Ljósavatnsskarð, ok svá til Mývatns, ok síðan Möðrudalsheiði".	"If you are curious of then, there shall i ride about Kjol to Skagafjord; then to Eyjafjord, from-there Ljosavatnsskard, and so to Mywater, and after Morudale-moor".	He turned back and said: "If you are curious then I shall ride around Kjol to Skagafjord, then to Eyafjord, and from there to Ljosavatnsskard and so on to Mywater, and after that Morudale-Moor".
Guðmundr mælti:	Gudmund said:	Gudmind said:
"Efn orð þín, ok ríð Ljósavatnsskarð".	"Carry-out words yours, and ride Ljosavatnsskard".	Carry out your words and ride through Ljosavatnsskard.
Broddi svarar:	Broddi said:	Broddi said:
"Efna skal þat; eðr ætlar þú, Guðmundr, at verja mér skarðit? Allmjök eru þér þá mislagðar hendr, ef þú varðar mér Ljósavatnsskarð, svá at ek mega þar eigi fara með förunautum mínum, enn þú varðar þat eigi, hit litla skarðit, sem er milli þjóa þér, svá at ámælilaust sé".	"Carry-out shall that; but intend you, Gudmund, to guard me the-pass All-greatly are you then misplaced hand, if you guard me Ljosavatnsskard, such that i may there not travel with companions mine, as you guarded that not, the little gap, as that between buttocks yours, so as without-reproach be".	"I shall carry that out, but do you intend to guard against me passing? You are greatly mistaken if you try to stop me at Ljosavatnsskard with my companions, as you failed to guard the little gap in your backside so as to be without reproach".
Skildist þeir við svá búit ok spurðust þessi orð um allt þingit.	Separated they with so settled and asked these words about all assembly.	They separated and these words were learnt by all who were at the assembly.
Enn er Þórkell Geitisson varð þess víss, þá gekk hann til fundar við Brodda, ok bað at hann skyldi ríða Sandleið, eðr ella hit eystra.	When that Thorkell Geitisson was this aware, then went he to meet with Brodda, and bid that he should ride Sandy-road, or otherwise the east.	When Thorkell Geitisson was aware of this, he went to meet with Broddi and invited that he "should ride on the sandy road or to the east".
Broddi svarar:	Broddi said:	Broddi said:
"Ek mun ríða þá leið, er ek hefi sagt Guðmundi, því at hann mun virða mér til hugleysis, ef ek fer eigi svá".	"I would ride then way, that i have said Gudmund, because that he should worth me to cowardice, if i travel not so".	I should ride the way that I told Gudmund I would, because otherwise he shall value me as a coward if I do not.

The Tale of Ale-Hood (Old Norse)

Old Norse	Literal	English
Þórkell mælti; "Vit munum þá riða báðir saman, frændi, ok flokkr okkarr litill".	Thorkell said; "With should then ride both together, kinsman, and band ours little".	Thorkell said: "We should both ride together then, kinsman, and our little band".
Broddi sagði, at honum þœtti sœmd í föruneyti hans, ok lézt þat gjarna vilja.	Broddi said, that he thought honour to companions his, and burden that remove would.	Broddi said that he thought it a great honour to ride with him and his companions, and it would remove a burden.
Síðan riða þeir Þórkell ok Broddi báðir saman með flokka sína norðr Öxnadalsheiði.	Afterwards rode they Thorkell and Broddi both together with band his north Oxnadale-moor.	Afterwards Thorkell and Broddi together with his band rode north to Oxnadale-Moor.
Váru þeir í einni ferð ok Einarr Eyjólfsson, mágr Þórkels.	Was they on one journey and Einar Eyjolfsson, brother-in-law Thorkell.	It was on the journey that Thorkell's father-in-law Einar Eyjolfsson joined them.
Riðu þeir Broddi ok Þórkell til Þverár, með Einari, ok váru þar um nótt.	Rode they Broddi and Thorkell to Thverriver, with Einar, and were there about night.	Broddi and Thorkell rode to Thverriver with Einar and stayed there for the night.
Síðan reið Einarr á leið með þeim með fjölmenni mikit, ok skildust eigi fyrr enn við Skjálfandafljót.	After riding Einar the way with them with followers many, and separated not before about with Skjalfandi-River.	Afterwards Einar and his many followers rode with them, and they did not separate until they reached Skjalfandi River.
Enn þeir Þórkell ok Broddi léttu eigi sinni ferð, fyrr enn þeir komu austr í Vápnafjörð til búa sinna.	About them Thorkell and Broddi relieved not their journey, before that they came east to Vopnafjord to homes theirs.	Einar then rode home and then Thorkell and Broddi did not rest their journey until they came east to Vapnfjord to their homes.
Þat sumar fór Þórkell at heimboði til Brodda frænda síns, ok þá þar allgóðar gjafir.	That summer travelled Thorkell to home-booth to Broddi kinsman his, and then there all-good gifts.	That summer Thorkell travelled to the home-booth of his kinsman Broddi and then accepted all good gifts.
Höfðu þeir þá hina bezta frændsemi með vináttu, ok helzt þat meðan þeir lifðu.	Had they then the best kinship with friendship, and held that long-as they lived.	They then had the best kinship as long as they lived.
Ok lýkr þar sögu Ölkofra.	And ends here the-saga Ale-Hood.	And here ends the saga of Ale-Hood.

Word List (Old Norse to English)

Old Norse	English

A, a

aðra	other, others
aðrir	other, others
af	from, of, of
afglapi	simpleton
aftaninn	back
aftr	back
alda	wave
aldr	age
aldri	aged
alla	all
allan	all, every
allfúss	all-happy, all-happy
allgóðar	all-good
allir	all, all
allmikit	all-much
allmjök	all-greatly, all-greatly, all-much, all-much
allr	all, all
allra	all
allt	all, all, altogether
allvesalliga	miserable
alþýðu	the-people
annan	next
annarr	another
annarri	another
annars	others
annat	other, other
annsvör	answer, answers
arga	a-dog's
at	as, as, at, at, of, of, that, that, the, the, to, to, to-you
attir	burned
auðsætt	obvious
augu	eyes
aumliga	abjectly
aumligast	miserable
austr	east, east

Á, á

á	about, at, by, during, in, is, of, on, river, the, to
ábyrgjast	guarantee
áðan	earlier
álnir	measures
ámælilaust	without-reproach
átt	had, owned
átti	had
áttu	directions, had, have
átzt	affection

Æ, æ

ætla	intend, suppose
ætlaði	intended
ætlar	intend

B, b

bað	asked, bid, invited
báðir	both
bæði	asked, both
baki	back
báru	bore
bauð	offered
beitast	employing
berusku	childishness
betr	better
betri	better
bezt	best
bezta	best
bezti	best
bíða	wait
biðja	ask
biðr	invited
birni	bear
Bjarnason	Bjarnason (name)
bjó	lived

Word List (Old Norse to English)

Old Norse	English
Bláskógum	Blawoods (place)
Böðvarsdal	Bodvarsdale (place)
borði	borne
brann	burned, burnt
brátt	soon, transformed
brendi	burned
brenna	burn
Brodda	Brodda (name), Brodda's (name), Broddi (name)
Brodd-Helgi	Brodd-Helgi (name)
Broddi	Broddi (name), drew
brott	away
brúarsporðinn	footbridge
brunnu	burned
brýn	urgent
búa	homes, settle
búða	booths
búðar	booth
búðarveggnum	booth-walls
búðina	booth
búðinni	booth, booths
búit	settled, to-settle
búizt	prepared
bust	cheated

D, d

Old Norse	English
dag	day
daga	days
daginn	the-day
deila	share, sharing
deildust	judged
dœma	deem
dœmdir	deem
drambi	arrogance
dregin	drawn
dregit	drawn
drengskapr	word-of-honour
drepa	kill
drepinn	killed
drifu	flocked
drjúgir	substantial
dró	drew
duga	help
dugit	enough
dugnað	assistance
dvaldist	dwelled
dylja	disguise
dýrligu	dearly

E, e

Old Norse	English
eðr	but, or
ef	if
efn	carry-out
efna	carry-out
eftir	after, behind, later
eftirförina	after-travelling
eiga	have
eigi	but, no, none, not, not-of, only
eigingirni	selfish
eign	may
eigu	have, own, said-of
ein	only
Einari	Einar (name)
Einarr	Einar (name)
einmæli	one-talk
einn	one
einni	one
einu	one
einurð	determined
Eirekssyni	Eriksson (name)
eitt	one
ek	and, i
ekki	not
ekkí	not
eldr	fire
eldrinn	fire
ella	otherwise
en	but
enda	in-the-end
engi	no, none
enn	about, and, as, but, in, than, that, the, then, when

Word List (Old Norse to English)

Old Norse	English
er	am, are, as, be, i, is, that, the, then, was, were, when, which, who
ert	are
eru	are, they, was, were
Eyjafjarðar	Eyjafjord (place)
Eyjólfr	Eyjolf (name)
Eyjólfsson	Eyjolfsson (name), son-of-Eyjolf (name)
eystra	east

F, f

Old Norse	English
fá	few
faðir	father
falli	fall
fallinn	fall
fangi	enemies
fara	travel
farir	travel
fastr	fastened
fé	fee, money
feginn	relieved
féit	fee
fekk	got
félaga	companions
feldr	fall
félitlir	fee-little
fell	fell
fengit	got
fer	go, travel
ferð	journey, travelled
ferr	go
festist	fastened
févænligt	money-promising
fimti	fifth
fingrum	fingers
firn	awful
fjandskap	fiend-ship
fjár	wealth
fjáreigandi	property-owning
fjarlægir	financial
fjölmenni	followers
fjórði	fourth

Old Norse	English
flokka	band
flokkr	band
föður	father
færi	opportunity
fæti	foot
fætrna	feet
fól	fool
fór	for, travelled
forðat	avoided
fórt	travelled
fóru	travelled
fórum	travelled
förunautar	companions
förunautum	companions
föruneyti	companions
forvitni	curious
fóta	feet
frá	from
frænda	kinsman, kinsmen
frændi	kinsman, kinsmen
frændsemi	kinship
fram	from
frammi	from-forward
fullting	assistance
fundar	meet
fundit	found
fúss	willing
fylgi	follow
fyrir	before, by, for, from, therefore
fyrr	before
fyrst	first

G, g

Old Norse	English
gæta	guarded
gæti	got
gáfu	gave
gagns	benefit
ganga	go, to-go, went
gefa	give
Geitisson	Geitisson (name), son-of-Geiti (name)
Geitissonar	Geitisson's (name)
gekk	got, went

Word List (Old Norse to English)

Old Norse	English
gellis	gellir
gengi	going
gengit	walked
gengu	none, went
gera	be, be-done, do, made, make, to-do
gerð	made
gerðar	do
gerði	did, done, made
gerðina	make
gerðinni	make
gerðist	happened, was
gerim	be, being, doing, make
gerist	was
gerit	make
gert	done
get	get
gettú	getting
gjafir	gifts
gjaldast	be-paid, pay
gjarna	remove
glámsýni	big-mistake
góð	good
góða	good
goðana	chieftans
goðar	chieftans, they
Goðaskógr	Godaskogur (place)
Goðdala-Starri	Guddala-Starri (name)
goði	chieftan
góðs	chieftans, good
góðu	good
göfigligri	nobler
goldit	paid
grátfeginn	weeping-for-joy
grét	wept
grimmu	grim
gripir	treasures
gröfunum	pit
Guðmund	Gudmund (name)
Guðmundar	Gudmund (name)
Guðmundi	Gudmund (name)
Guðmundr	Gudmund (name)

H, h

Old Norse	English
hætta	end
hafa	have
hafði	had, he
hafim	have
hafir	have
hafit	have
hagr	handy
halanum	tail-wagging
halda	hold
Hallsson	Hallsson (name)
handlaginu	agreement, handshake
handsala	confirm
handsals-vætti	agreement
hann	he, him, it
hans	him, his
hátt	way
haust	autumn
haustit	autumn
hefði	had
hefi	have
hefir	has, have
hefna	revenge
hefnir	avenge
heim	home
heimboði	home-booth
heita	call
heiti	named
heitinn	named
heldr	rather
helzt	held
hendr	hand
hér	he, here
heraða	districts
heruð	district, districts
hestrinn	horse
hét	was-named
hina	the, then
hinir	other
hinn	the
hinum	others
hit	the, then
hitt	find, found

Word List (Old Norse to English)

Old Norse	English
hittast	meet
hitti	found
hittust	found
hjá	beside
hjálpa	help
hjálpit	help
hljóp	ran
hlut	lot
hluta	lot
hlýða	listen
hnœfilyrðum	blows
hœttir	mannered
höfði	head
höfðingja	chieftans
höfðingjarnir	chieftans
höfðu	had, owned
höfum	have
honum	he, him, his, to-him
hræddr	scared
Hrafnabjörgum	Hrafnabjorg (place)
hrapa	hurry
hraunit	lava-fields
hraustr	brave
hug	mind
hugleysis	cowardice
hún	she
hvaðan	where
hvar	where
hvárt	either, whether, which
hvass	sharp
hverja	what
hverjum	each, whether
hverr	who
hvers	each
hversu	how, how-so
hveru	each
hyggja	think

I, i

Old Norse	English
i	of, to
iðju	occupation
iðn	craft
illa	ill
illt	ill
illyrðum	malice
inn	in

Í, í

Old Norse	English
í	about, among, as, at, in, of, on, that, the, to, with
íþróttamaðr	sports-man

J, j

Old Norse	English
jafnan	equally
jafnstórliga	equally-great
jarðar	earth
járn	iron

K, k

Old Norse	English
kæra	accuse
kalla	call
kallaðr	called
kallat	called
kann	can, known
kápuna	cloak
kastaði	cast
kastar	cast
kaup	bought, buy
kaupa	bought, buy
kemr	come
kenna	know
keypt	bought
keyptu	bought
Kjöl	Kjol (place)
kjörir	choice
kjörit	choice
kjósa	choose
klengisök	small-blame
kœmi	came
kofra	hood
kol	coal
kola	coal
kolbrennu	coal-burning

Word List (Old Norse to English)

Old Norse	English
kölluðu	called
kom	came
koma	came, come, coming
kominn	coming
komit	comes, coming
komnir	coming
komu	came
komumst	come
konu	wife
kost	benefit
kostr	choice
kraup	kneeled
kunna	know
kvað	said
kveðjum	greet
kýs	choose

L, l

Old Norse	English
lætr	behaviour
lagði	laid
lagðist	laid
lagt	laid
láta	leave, let
látim	let
látum	let-us
launanna	loans
leggja	allow
leggr	lay
leið	the, way
leita	objection
leitar	seek
leitat	sought
lengi	long, longer
lét	let
léttra	easier
léttu	relieved
lézt	burden, let
lið	assistance, company, help
líða	passed
liði	help
liðs	assistance, help, people
liðveizlunni	supportive
lifðu	lived
liggir	laying
líkar	alike
líkast	likely
limit	foliage
litill	little, small
litilræði	little-advised
lítils	little
litla	little
lítt	little
lízt	beholding, like
Ljósavatnsskarð	Ljosavatnsskard (place)
ljótr	ugly
lofar	praises
lög	law
lög-(sögu)maðr	law-speaker
logaði	blazed
Lögbergi	Law-Rock (place)
Lögbergs	Law-Rock (place)
lögréttu	law-assembly
lögréttuna	law-assembly
lögskil	legal-settlement
lokit	ended
Lönguhlið	Langahlid (place)
lúka	finish
lúkim	conclude
lýkr	ends
lykt	conclusion
lýsa	show
lýsír	declared

M, m

Old Norse	English
má	may
maðr	a-man, man
mæla	matters
mælir	speaks, talking
mælti	said, spoke
mág	brother-in-law
mágr	brother-in-law
mál	matter, matter, the-matter
málaefni	matters
máli	matter, speak

Word List (Old Norse to English)

Old Norse	English
málinu	case
málit	matter, the-matter
málkunnigr	talking-known
málóði	of-strong-language
máls	matter
mann	man
manna	men
mannamunr	integrity
manni	man
manns	man's
mannsektir	fines
mansöngsdrápu	love-song-poem
marga	many
margir	many
margt	many
markaði	marked
mátti	may
máttir	may
með	among, it, with
meðan	long-as
mega	may
meira	more
menn	man, many, men, people
mér	i, me, of-me, to, to-me, you
merarlíki	mare-like
merin	mare
mest	most
mik	me
mikil	much
mikit	many
miklir	great
milli	between
mín	mine
mína	mine
minn	mine
minni	mine
minnisamt	memorable
mínu	my
mínum	mine
misjafnt	uneven-in
mislagðar	misplaced
missmíði	mistake
missýni	mistake
missýnist	mistake
mitt	my
mjök	much
Möðrudalsheiði	Morudale-moor (place)
mögr	skinny
mönnum	men
mörgum	many
mun	shall, should, would
mundi	could, would
mundu	would
mungátin	ale
muni	would
munir	should
munngát	ale
muntú	should
munu	shall, should, will
munum	should
mútugjafir	bribes
Mývatns	Mywater (place)

N, n

Old Norse	English
næða	neared
næst	nearest, next
næsta	next-to
næstir	nearest
nafn	name
nafnfrægr	named
nafni	the-name
nefi	nose, noses
nefndi	named
nefndir	name
nefndr	named
neitaða	refusal, refused
nema	take, taking
niðrfall	dropping
nökkura	some
nökkurar	some
nökkurir	some
nökkurn	someone
nökkuru	somewhat
nökkut	some, something
norðr	north
nótt	night
nóttina	night

Word List (Old Norse to English)

Old Norse	English
nú	not, now
nytja	use

O, o

Old Norse	English
ofan	over
ofarliga	high-up
ofreflismenn	ultra-strong-men
oft	often
oftliga	often
ok	also, and
okkarr	ours
okkart	ours
okkr	ours, us
okkra	ours
orð	word, words
orða	words
orðinn	become
orðit	word
orðum	words
ormr	orm
ortir	worded
oss	ours, us, we

Ó, ó

Old Norse	English
ógæfu	un-giving
óhœfan	trouble
ólíkligt	unlike
ómakligr	uncomfortable
ópit	open
ór	from, of, out-of
órhjarta	un-heartened
óvinum	un-friends
óvizku	unwise

Ö, ö

Old Norse	English
öðrum	other, others
öl	ale
Ölkofra	Ale-Hood (name), Ale-hood's (name)
Ölkofri	Ale-Hood (name)
öll	all
öllu	all
önnur	another
Öxnadalsheiði	Oxnadale-moor (place)
öxnina	oxen
öxnum	oxen

Œ, œ

Old Norse	English
œrr	awed

R, r

Old Norse	English
ráð	advice, matter
ráði	counsel
ráðinn	decided
ráðit	decided
ræddi	discussed
rakkara	bolder
ráku	drove
rán	robbery
rann	runs
rattlátir	right-like
Rauða-Bjarnarson	son-of-Rauda-Bjarn (name)
regin	ruling
reið	riding, rode, travelled
reiðasti	most-angry
reiðst	counsel
reikuðu	roamed
reitt	riding, rode
reytti	tried
ríð	ride
riða	ride, rode
ríða	ride
riðu	rode
rœddu	discussed

S, s

Old Norse	English
sá	saw, so, that, this
sæli	good

Word List (Old Norse to English)

Old Norse	English	Old Norse	English
sæll	happy	sitja	sit
sætt	settlement	sjá	saw, this
saga	story	sjálfdæmi	self-judgement
sagði	said	sjálfdœmi	self-judgement
sagt	said, told	sjálfr	himself, yourself
sakferlum	lawsuits	sjúkr	stingy
sama	same	skaða	damages
saman	together	Skafta	Skafti (name)
sandleið	sandy-road	Skafti	Skafti (name)
sanns	the-truth	Skagafjarðar	Skagafjord (place)
sat	sat	skal	shall
satt	TRUE	skalt	shall
sátt	settlement	skaltu	shall-you
sáttu	saw-you	skaltú	shall-you
sátu	sat	skarð	gap
sé	as, be, being, see, should, so	skarðit	gap, the-pass
segir	said	skáru	cut
segja	said, say	skatt	tax
seint	late	skerða	action
sekja	seek	skifta	exchange
sektar	guilt	skildist	separated
seldu	sold	skildust	separated
selfeitan	fat	skilit	divided, understood
selja	sell	skilt	divided
sem	as, me, so, that, which	Skjálfandafljót	Skjalfandi-River (place)
sendi	sent	sköðum	damage
sendiboð	messenger, sending-asked	skóg	forest
sér	him, himself, his, themselves	skóga	forest
		skógabrennuna	forest-burning
sérhverjum	theirs	skógana	forest, forests
sétti	sixth	skógar	forests
sex	six	skógarmanns	outlawry
siðan	then	skóggangssök	outlawry
síðan	after, afterwards, since, then	skóginn	forest
		skógr	forest
siðr	custom	skulu	shall, should
Síðu-Hallssonar	son-of-Sidu-Hall (name)	skylda	should
		skyldi	should, wished
sín	theirs	skyldim	should
sína	his, their	skyldu	should
sinn	his	skylim	should
sinna	theirs	skýrst	clarified
sinni	his, opinion, their	skýrt	clear
síns	his	slík	such
		slíka	such

Word List (Old Norse to English)

Old Norse	English
slikt	such
slíkt	so, such
slíkum	such
slitu	dissolved
slöðraði	trailing-behind
sneri	turned
snökta	sob
Snorri	Snorri (name)
snýr	turned
sœmd	honour
sœmdunum	honour
sofnaði	slept
sögðu	said
sögðust	said
sögu	the-saga
sögunni	the-saga
sökina	seeking
sökum	blame
sökunautr	defendant
son	son
spurði	asked
spurðust	asked
spurt	asked
staðfest	confirmed
stalt	stealing
Starri	Starri (name)
stefnda	summonsed
stefndi	summons
stefnuför	summons
Steingrimr	Steingrim (name)
stikat	stitched
stóð	stood
stóðhest	stallion
stórlæti	pride
stórleika	pride
stórmenni	great-men
stórorðr	high-sounding
stúf	stump
stundir	awhile
stundu	awhile
stungizt	wounded
sú	yours
sumar	summer
sumarit	summer
sundr	asunder
svá	saying, so, such
svarar	answered, said
sverð	sword
Svíðingi	Svidning (place)
svöruðu	answered
svörum	answers
synjat	refused

T, t

Old Norse	English
taka	take
takast	took
talaða	said
telja	tell
tíðinda	news
tíðindi	news
til	about, for, little, to
tiltœkilegt	available
tíma	time
tœki	took
tók	took
tré	wood
trefill	trefill
tvá	two
tvítugs	twenty

Þ, þ

Old Norse	English
þá	so, then, there, you
þaðan	from-there
þakksamliga	thankfully
þann	that
þar	here, that, there
þarfnast	as-needed
þat	it, that, the, this, to, with
þau	his, they
Þórðarson	Thordarson (name)
Þórkels	Thorkell (name)
þegar	as-soon-as, straightaway, straight-away, then
þeim	them, they, those

Word List (Old Norse to English)

Old Norse	English	*Old Norse*	English
þeir	chieftans, them, they, this	Þórsteins	Thorstein (name), Thorstein's (name)
þeira	of-the, their, theirs, them, these, they, those	þótt	though, thought
		þótti	seem, seemed
		þóttist	thought
þeiri	their	þriði	third
þenna	that, this	þú	you, your
þér	that, then, to-you, you, yours	þung	heavy
		þungs	heavily
þess	this	þurfa	need
þessa	then, this	þurfu	need
þessar	this	Þverár	Thverriver (place)
þessi	so, these, this	þverr	around
þessir	these	því	as, because, for, of, since, that, then, therefore, what, why, with
þessu	these, this		
þetta	it, that, this		
þiggja	receive		
þik	you	þykki	think
þín	yours	þykkir	seems
þingi	assembly	þykkjast	consider
þingit	assembly		
þinglausnir	assembly-ending		
þingmenn	assembly, assembly-men	# U, u	
þings	assembly	um	about, around, in, of, over
þingum	assembly	undir	from-beneath, under
þinn	you, yours	upp	up
þinni	yours		
þíns	your, yours	# Ú, ú	
þit	you		
þitt	yours	út	from, out, out-of
þjóa	buttocks		
þó	then, though	# V, v	
þœtti	thought		
þoli	tolerate	váðaverk	accidents
Þórðar	Thord (name)	vaðmál	homespun-cloth
Þórhallr	Thorhall (name)	vænta	expect
Þórhallsstöðum	Thorhallsstead (place)	væra	would-be
		væri	was, were, would-be
þori	greater-part	vaknaði	awoke
Þórkel	Thorkell (name)	vakti	woke
Þórkeli	Thorkell (name)	ván	hope, wished
Þórkell	Thorkell (name)	vandast	difficult
Þórkels	Thorkell (name)	vanir	friends
Þórstein	Thorstein (name)		
Þórsteinn	Thorstein (name)		

Word List (Old Norse to English)

Old Norse	English
Vápnafjörð	Vopnafjord (place)
var	then, was, were
vár	are, spring
varaðist	warned
varð	became, was, were
varða	concerning
varðar	guard, guarded
varðtú	were-you
varit	defend
várkunn	pity
várr	our
várra	talking-loudly
vart	were
várþings	local-assembly
váru	was, were
varut	were
Vatnsdal	Vatnsdal (place)
vátta	witness
váttar	witnesses
váttnefna	witnesses
veg	way
veginn	killed
vegr	way
veifiskati	spendthrift
veik	gave
veit	know
veita	grant, know, provide
veitit	know
veitti	granted
veittú	grant
vel	well
vér	on, we
vera	be
verð	deserve
verða	being, was, were
verðr	worth
verit	been
verja	guard
verr	worse
verri	worsen
vert	worth
vestr	west
vetrinn	winter
við	with
víða	many, widely
viðinn	trees
vil	will
vilda	willed
vildi	willed, wills
vili	willing
vilit	will
vilja	willed, wish, would
viljum	will
vill	will, wishes
vilnat	willed
vináttu	friendship
vindr	wind
vini	friends
vinir	friends
vinsæl	popularity
virða	worth
virðir	value
víss	aware
vit	we, with
vitrir	wise
vitu	knowing
völluna	plains

Y, y

Old Norse	English
yðr	yours
yðra	yours
yðrum	yours
yðvarn	your
yfir	across, over
ykkr	you
yppa	up
yrði	be

Word List *(English to Old Norse)*

English	Old Norse	English	Old Norse
		among	*í, í*
A, a		accuse	*kæra*
		allow	*leggja*
about	*á, á, á, á, á*	alike	*líkar*
at	*á, á, á, á*	a-man	*maðr*
age	*aldr*	ale	*mungátin, munngát, mútugjafir*
aged	*aldri*		
all	*alla, allan, allan, allfúss, allfúss, allgóðar, allir, allir, allmikit, allmjök, allmjök*	awed	*œrr*
		also	*ok*
		Ale-Hood (name)	*Ölkofra, Ölkofra*
		Ale-hood's (name)	*Ölkofra*
		advice	*ráð*
all-happy	*allfúss, allfúss*	afterwards	*síðan*
all-good	*allgóðar*	action	*skerða*
all-much	*allmikit, allmjök, allmjök*	awhile	*stundir, stundu*
		asunder	*sundr*
all-greatly	*allmjök, allmjök*	answered	*svarar, svöruðu*
altogether	*allt*	as-needed	*þarfnast*
another	*annarr, annarri, annsvör*	as-soon-as	*þegar*
		assembly	*þingi, þingit, þinglausnir, þingmenn, þingmenn*
answer	*annsvör*		
answers	*annsvör, arga*	assembly-ending	*þinglausnir*
a-dog's	*arga*	assembly-men	*þingmenn*
as	*at, at, at, at, átt, átti, attir, áttu*	around	*þverr, því*
		available	*tiltœkilegt*
affection	*átzt*	accidents	*váðaverk*
abjectly	*aumliga*	awoke	*vaknaði*
asked	*bað, bað, bað, báðir, bæði*	aware	*víss*
		across	*yfir*
ask	*biðja*		
away	*brott*	**B, b**	
arrogance	*drambi*		
assistance	*dugnað, dvaldist, dylja, dýrligu*	by	*á, á*
		back	*aftaninn, aftr, aldr*
after	*eftir, eftir*	burned	*attir, áttu, áttu, áttu*
after-travelling	*eftirförina*	bid	*bað*
and	*ek, ek, eldr*	both	*báðir, bæði*
am	*er*	bore	*báru*
are	*er, er, er, er*	better	*betr, betri*
awful	*firn*	best	*bezt, bezta, bezti*
avoided	*forðat*	bear	*birni*
agreement	*handlaginu, handlaginu*		
autumn	*haust, haustit*		
avenge	*hefnir*		

Word List (English to Old Norse)

English	Old Norse
Bjarnason (name)	*Bjarnason*
Blawoods (place)	*Bláskógum*
Bodvarsdale (place)	*Böðvarsdal*
borne	*borði*
burnt	*brann*
burn	*brenna*
Brodda (name)	*Brodda*
Brodda's (name)	*Brodda*
Broddi (name)	*Brodda, Brodd-Helgi*
Brodd-Helgi (name)	*Brodd-Helgi*
booths	*búða, búðar*
booth	*búðar, búðarveggnum, búðina*
booth-walls	*búðarveggnum*
but	*eðr, ef, efn, efna*
behind	*eftir*
be	*er, er, er, ert, eru, Eyjafjarðar*
band	*flokka, flokkr*
before	*fyrir, fyrir*
benefit	*gagns, ganga*
be-done	*gera*
being	*gerim, gerim, gerim*
be-paid	*gjaldast*
big-mistake	*glámsýni*
beside	*hjá*
blows	*hnœfilyrðum*
brave	*hraustr*
bought	*kaup, kaup, kaupa, kaupa*
buy	*kaup, kaupa*
behaviour	*lætr*
burden	*lézt*
beholding	*lízt*
blazed	*logaði*
brother-in-law	*mág, mágr*
between	*milli*
bribes	*mútugjafir*
become	*orðinn*
bolder	*rakkara*
blame	*sökum*
buttocks	*þjóa*
because	*því*
became	*varð*
been	*verit*

C, c

English	Old Norse
childishness	*berusku*
cheated	*bust*
carry-out	*efn, efna*
companions	*félaga, feldr, félitlir, fell*
curious	*forvitni*
chieftans	*goðana, goðar, Goðaskógr, Goðdala-Starri, goði, góðs*
chieftan	*goði*
confirm	*handsala*
call	*heita, helzt*
cowardice	*hugleysis*
craft	*iðn*
called	*kallaðr, kallat, kann*
can	*kann*
cloak	*kápuna*
cast	*kastaði, kastar*
come	*kemr, kenna, keypt*
choice	*kjörir, kjörit, kjósa*
choose	*kjósa, kœmi*
came	*kœmi, kofra, kol, kola*
coal	*kol, kola*
coal-burning	*kolbrennu*
coming	*koma, kominn, komit, komit*
comes	*komit*
company	*lið*
conclude	*lúkim*
conclusion	*lykt*
case	*málinu*
could	*mundi*
counsel	*ráði, ráðinn*
custom	*siðr*
cut	*skáru*
clarified	*skýrst*
clear	*skýrt*
confirmed	*staðfest*
consider	*þykkjast*
concerning	*varða*

Word List (English to Old Norse)

English	Old Norse	English	Old Norse

D, d

during	*á*
directions	*áttu*
drew	*broddi, brott*
day	*dag*
days	*daga*
deem	*dœma, dœmdir*
drawn	*dregin, dregit*
dwelled	*dvaldist*
disguise	*dylja*
dearly	*dýrligu*
determined	*einurð*
do	*gera, gera*
did	*gerði*
done	*gerði, gerði*
doing	*gerim*
districts	*heraða, heruð*
district	*heruð*
declared	*lýsír*
dropping	*niðrfall*
decided	*ráðinn, ráðit*
discussed	*ræddi, rakkara*
drove	*ráku*
damages	*skaða*
divided	*skilit, skilt*
damage	*sköðum*
dissolved	*slitu*
defendant	*sökunautr*
difficult	*vandast*
defend	*varit*
deserve	*verð*

E, e

earlier	*áðan*
every	*allan*
eyes	*augu*
east	*austr, austr, bað*
employing	*beitast*
enough	*dugit*
Einar (name)	*Einari, Einarr*
Eriksson (name)	*Eirekssyni*
Eyjafjord (place)	*Eyjafjarðar*
Eyjolf (name)	*Eyjólfr*
Eyjolfsson (name)	*Eyjólfsson*
enemies	*fangi*
end	*hætta*
either	*hvárt*
each	*hverjum, hvers, hversu*
equally	*jafnan*
equally-great	*jafnstórliga*
earth	*jarðar*
easier	*léttra*
ended	*lokit*
ends	*lýkr*
exchange	*skifta*
expect	*vænta*

F, f

from	*af, aftaninn, aftr, aldr, aldri, alla*
footbridge	*brúarsporðinn*
flocked	*drifu*
fire	*eldr, eldrinn*
few	*fá*
father	*faðir, falli*
fall	*falli, fallinn, fangi*
fastened	*fastr, fé*
fee	*fé, fé*
fee-little	*félitlir*
fell	*fell*
fifth	*fimti*
fingers	*fingrum*
fiend-ship	*fjandskap*
financial	*fjarlægir*
followers	*fjölmenni*
fourth	*fjórði*
foot	*fœti*
feet	*fœtrna, fól*
fool	*fól*
for	*fór, forðat, förunautar, förunautum*
from-forward	*frammi*
found	*fundit, fylgi, fyrir, fyrir*
follow	*fylgi*
first	*fyrst*

Word List (English to Old Norse)

English	Old Norse	English	Old Norse
find	*hitt*	greater-part	*þori*
foliage	*limit*	guard	*varðar, varðar*
finish	*lúka*	grant	*veita, veita*
fines	*mannsektir*	granted	*veitti*
fat	*selfeitan*		
forest	*skóg, skóga, skógabrennuna, skógana, skógana*		

H, h

English	Old Norse
had	*átt, átti, attir, áttu, áttu, áttu*
have	*áttu, átzt, augu, aumliga, aumligast, austr, austr, bað, bað, bað*
homes	*búa*
help	*duga, dugit, dugnað, dvaldist, dylja, dýrligu*
happened	*gerðist*
he	*hafði, hafim, hafir, hafit*
handy	*hagr*
hold	*halda*
Hallsson (name)	*Hallsson*
handshake	*handlaginu*
him	*hann, hann, hans, hans*
his	*hans, haust, haustit, hefði, hefi, hefir, hefir, hefnir*
has	*hefir*
home	*heim*
home-booth	*heimboði*
held	*helzt*
hand	*hendr*
here	*hér, heraða*
horse	*hestrinn*
head	*höfði*
Hrafnabjorg (place)	*Hrafnabjörgum*
hurry	*hrapa*
how	*hversu*
how-so	*hversu*
hood	*kofra*
high-up	*ofarliga*
happy	*sæll*
himself	*sér, sér*
honour	*sœmd, sœmdunum*
high-sounding	*stórorðr*

English	Old Norse
forest-burning	*skógabrennuna*
forests	*skógana, skógar*
from-there	*þaðan*
from-beneath	*undir*
friends	*vanir, vár, varð*
friendship	*vináttu*

G, g

English	Old Norse
guarantee	*ábyrgjast*
got	*fekk, félaga, feldr, félitlir*
go	*fer, ferð, ferr*
guarded	*gæta, gæti*
gave	*gáfu, gagns*
give	*gefa*
Geitisson (name)	*Geitisson*
Geitisson's (name)	*Geitissonar*
gellir	*gellis*
going	*gengi*
get	*get*
getting	*gettú*
gifts	*gjafir*
good	*góð, góða, goðana, goðar, Goðaskógr*
Godaskogur (place)	*Goðaskógr*
Guddala-Starri (name)	*Goðdala-Starri*
grim	*grimmu*
Gudmund (name)	*Guðmund, Guðmundar, Guðmundi, Guðmundr*
greet	*kveðjum*
great	*miklir*
guilt	*sektar*
gap	*skarð, skarðit*
great-men	*stórmenni*

Word List (English to Old Norse)

English	*Old Norse*
heavy	*þung*
heavily	*þungs*
homespun-cloth	*vaðmál*
hope	*ván*

I, i

English	*Old Norse*
in	*á, á, ábyrgjast, áðan, ætla*
is	*á, ábyrgjast*
intend	*ætla, ætlaði*
intended	*ætlaði*
invited	*bað, báðir*
if	*ef*
i	*ek, eldr, eldrinn*
in-the-end	*enda*
it	*hann, hans, hans, haust*
ill	*illa, illt*
iron	*járn*
integrity	*mannamunr*

J, j

English	*Old Norse*
judged	*deildust*
journey	*ferð*

K, k

English	*Old Norse*
kill	*drepa*
killed	*drepinn, drifu*
kinsman	*frænda, frænda*
kinsmen	*frænda, frændi*
kinship	*frændsemi*
known	*kann*
know	*kenna, keypt, keyptu, Kjöl, kjörir*
Kjol (place)	*Kjöl*
kneeled	*kraup*
knowing	*vitu*

L, l

English	*Old Norse*
lived	*bjó, Bláskógum*
later	*eftir*
lot	*hlut, hluta*
listen	*hlýða*
lava-fields	*hraunit*
laid	*lagði, lagðist, lagt*
leave	*láta*
let	*láta, látim, látum, launanna*
let-us	*látum*
loans	*launanna*
lay	*leggr*
long	*lengi*
longer	*lengi*
laying	*liggir*
likely	*líkast*
little	*litill, litilræði, lítils, litla, lítt*
little-advised	*litilræði*
like	*lízt*
Ljosavatnsskard (place)	*Ljósavatnsskarð*
law	*lög*
law-speaker	*lög-(sögu)maðr*
Law-Rock (place)	*Lögbergi, Lögbergs*
law-assembly	*lögréttu, lögréttuna*
legal-settlement	*lögskil*
Langahlid (place)	*Lönguhlið*
love-song-poem	*mansöngsdrápu*
long-as	*meðan*
lawsuits	*sakferlum*
late	*seint*
local-assembly	*várþings*

M, m

English	*Old Norse*
miserable	*allvesalliga, álnir*
measures	*álnir*
may	*eign, eigu, Einari, Einarr, einurð*
money	*fé*
money-promising	*févænligt*
meet	*fundar, fundit*

Word List (English to Old Norse)

English	Old Norse	English	Old Norse
made	gera, gera, gerð	named	heiti, heitinn, heldr, hét, hina
make	gera, gerð, gerðar, gerði, gerði	neared	næða
mannered	hœttir	nearest	næst, næst
mind	hug	next-to	næsta
malice	illyrðum	name	nafn, nafnfrægr
man	maðr, mæla, mág, mágr	nose	nefi
matters	mæla, mág	noses	nefi
matter	mál, mál, málaefni, máli, málinu, málit	north	norðr
men	manna, mannamunr, manni	night	nótt, nóttina
		now	nú
man's	manns	need	þurfa, þurfu
many	marga, margir, margt, markaði, mátti, máttir, með	news	tíðinda, tíðindi

O, o

English	Old Norse
marked	markaði
more	meira
me	mér, merarlíki, merin
mare-like	merarlíki
mare	merin
most	mest
much	mikil, mikit
mine	mín, mína, minn, minni, minnisamt
memorable	minnisamt
my	mínu, mínum
misplaced	mislagðar
mistake	missmíði, missýni, missýnist
Morudale-moor (place)	Möðrudalsheiði
Mywater (place)	Mývatns
most-angry	reiðasti
messenger	sendiboð

English	Old Norse
of	á, á, á, á, á, aðra, aðra, aðrir, aðrir, ætla
on	á, á, á
other	aðra, aðra, aðrir, aðrir, ætla, af
others	aðra, aðrir, aðrir, ætla, af
owned	átt, auðsætt
obvious	auðsætt
offered	bauð
or	eðr
only	eigi, eigingirni
own	eigu
one-talk	einmæli
one	einn, einni, einu, eitt
otherwise	ella
opportunity	fœri
occupation	iðju
objection	leita
of-strong-language	málóði
of-me	mér
over	ofan, ofreflismenn, oft
often	oft, oftliga
ours	okkarr, okkart, okkr, okkr, okkra
open	ópit
out-of	ór, orð
orm	ormr
Oxnadale-moor (place)	Öxnadalsheiði

N, n

English	Old Norse
next	annan, annars
no	eigi, eigi
none	eigi, eigi, eigi
not	eigi, eigi, eigi, eigingirni
not-of	eigi
nobler	göfigligri

Word List (English to Old Norse)

English	*Old Norse*	English	*Old Norse*
oxen	*öxnina, öxnum*		
opinion	*sinni*		
outlawry	*skógarmanns, skóggangssök*		
of-the	*þeira*		
out	*út*		
our	*várr*		

P, p

prepared	*búizt*		
property-owning	*fjáreigandi*		
pay	*gjaldast*		
paid	*goldit*		
pit	*gröfunum*		
passed	*líða*		
people	*liðs, liðveizlunni*		
praises	*lofar*		
pride	*stórlæti, stórleika*		
pity	*várkunn*		
provide	*veita*		
popularity	*vinsæl*		
plains	*völluna*		

R, r

river	*á*
relieved	*feginn, fer*
remove	*gjarna*
revenge	*hefna*
rather	*heldr*
ran	*hljóp*
refusal	*neitaða*
refused	*neitaða, nema*
robbery	*rán*
runs	*rann*
right-like	*ráttlátir*
ruling	*regin*
riding	*reið, reið*
rode	*reið, reið, reikuðu, reitt*
roamed	*reikuðu*
ride	*ríð, riða, riða*
receive	*þiggja*

S, s

suppose	*ætla*
simpleton	*afglapi*
soon	*brátt*
settle	*búa*
settled	*búit*
share	*deila*
sharing	*deila*
substantial	*drjúgir*
selfish	*eigingirni*
said-of	*eigu*
son-of-Eyjolf (name)	*Eyjólfsson*
son-of-Geiti (name)	*Geitisson*
scared	*hræddr*
she	*hún*
sharp	*hvass*
sports-man	*íþróttamaðr*
small-blame	*klengisök*
said	*kvað, leið, leið, leita, leitar, leitat, léttu, líða, liðs, liðveizlunni*
seek	*leitar, leitat*
sought	*leitat*
supportive	*liðveizlunni*
small	*litill*
show	*lýsa*
speaks	*mælir*
spoke	*mælti*
speak	*máli*
skinny	*mögr*
shall	*mun, mun, mun, mundi, mundu*
should	*mun, mun, mundi, mundu, muni, munir, muntú, munu, munu, munu, munum, næða*
some	*nökkura, nökkurar, nökkurir, nökkurn*
someone	*nökkurn*
somewhat	*nökkuru*
something	*nökkut*
son-of-Rauda-Bjarn (name)	*Rauða-Bjarnarson*
saw	*sá, sá*

Word List (English to Old Norse)

English	*Old Norse*	English	*Old Norse*
so	*sá, sá, sá, sætt, saga, sagði, sagt*	sword	*sverð*
settlement	*sætt, saga*	Svidning (place)	*Svíðingi*
story	*saga*	straightaway	*þegar*
same	*sama*	straight-away	*þegar*
sandy-road	*sandleið*	seem	*þótti*
sat	*sat, satt*	seemed	*þótti*
saw-you	*sáttu*	seems	*þykkir*
see	*sé*	spring	*vár*
say	*segja*	spendthrift	*veifiskati*
sold	*seldu*		
sell	*selja*		
sent	*sendi*		
sending-asked	*sendiboð*		
sixth	*sétti*		
six	*sex*		
since	*síðan, síðan*		
son-of-Sidu-Hall (name)	*Síðu-Hallssonar*		
sit	*sitja*		
self-judgement	*sjálfdæmi, sjálfdœmi*		
stingy	*sjúkr*		
Skafti (name)	*Skafta, Skafti*		
Skagafjord (place)	*Skagafjarðar*		
shall-you	*skaltu, skaltú*		
separated	*skildist, skildust*		
Skjalfandi-River (place)	*Skjálfandafljót*		
such	*slík, slíka, slikt, slíkt, slíkt, slíkum*		
sob	*snökta*		
Snorri (name)	*Snorri*		
slept	*sofnaði*		
seeking	*sökina*		
son	*son*		
stealing	*stalt*		
Starri (name)	*Starri*		
summonsed	*stefnda*		
summons	*stefndi, stefnuför*		
Steingrim (name)	*Steingrimr*		
stitched	*stikat*		
stood	*stóð*		
stallion	*stóðhest*		
stump	*stúf*		
summer	*sumar, sumarit*		
saying	*svá*		

T, t

English	*Old Norse*
the	*á, á, aðra, aðra, aðrir, aðrir, ætla, af, af, afglapi, alda*
to	*á, aðra, aðra, aðrir, aðrir, ætla, af, af*
the-people	*alþýðu*
that	*at, at, at, at, at, at, at, átt, auðsætt, bauð, bíða, brátt, brátt, brýn*
to-you	*at, átt*
transformed	*brátt*
to-settle	*búit*
the-day	*daginn*
than	*enn*
then	*enn, enn, er, er, er, er, er, er, er, er, eru, eru, eru*
they	*eru, eru, eru, Eyjólfsson, fara, farir*
travel	*fara, farir, feginn*
travelled	*ferð, fjár, fjáreigandi, fœri, fór, fórt*
therefore	*fyrir, ganga*
to-go	*ganga*
to-do	*gera*
treasures	*gripir*
tail-wagging	*halanum*
to-him	*honum*
think	*hyggja, i*
talking	*mælir*
the-matter	*mál, máli*
talking-known	*málkunnigr*
to-me	*mér*
the-name	*nafni*

Word List (English to Old Norse)

English	Old Norse	English	Old Norse
take	*nema, nema*	two	*tvá*
taking	*nema*	twenty	*tvítugs*
trouble	*óhœfan*	talking-loudly	*várra*
tried	*reytti*	trees	*viðinn*
this	*sá, sætt, saga, sagði, sagt, sagt, sama, saman, sandleið, sanns, sat*		

U, u

English	Old Norse
told	*sagt*
together	*saman*
the-truth	*sanns*
true	
themselves	*sér*
theirs	*sérhverjum, sétti, sex, siðan*
their	*sína, sinna, sinni, sinni*
the-pass	*skarðit*
tax	*skatt*
trailing-behind	*slöðraði*
turned	*sneri, snökta*
the-saga	*sögu, sögunni*
took	*takast, talaða, telja*
tell	*telja*
there	*þá, þá*
thankfully	*þakksamliga*
Thordarson (name)	*Þórðarson*
Thorkell (name)	*Þórkels, þegar, þegar, þegar, þeim*
them	*þeim, þeim, þeim*
those	*þeim, þeir*
these	*þeira, þeira, þeira, þeiri*
though	*þó, þœtti*
thought	*þœtti, þoli, Þórðar*
tolerate	*þoli*
Thord (name)	*Þórðar*
Thorhall (name)	*Þórhallr*
Thorhallsstead (place)	*Þórhallsstöðum*
Thorstein (name)	*Þórstein, Þórsteinn, Þórsteins*
Thorstein's (name)	*Þórsteins*
third	*þriði*
Thverriver (place)	*Þverár*
time	*tíma*
trefill	*trefill*

English	Old Norse
urgent	*brýn*
ugly	*ljótr*
uneven-in	*misjafnt*
use	*nytja*
ultra-strong-men	*ofreflismenn*
un-giving	*ógæfu*
us	*okkr, okkra*
unlike	*ólíkligt*
uncomfortable	*ómakligr*
un-heartened	*órhjarta*
un-friends	*óvinum*
unwise	*óvizku*
understood	*skilit*
under	*undir*
up	*upp, út*

V, v

English	Old Norse
Vopnafjord (place)	*Vápnafjörð*
Vatnsdal (place)	*Vatnsdal*
value	*virðir*

W, w

English	Old Norse
wave	*alda*
without-reproach	*ámælilaust*
wait	*bíða*
word-of-honour	*drengskapr*
when	*enn, er*
was	*er, er, er, er, er, eru, eru, eru, Eyjólfsson*
were	*er, er, er, er, eru, eru, eru, Eyjólfsson, fara*
which	*er, er, eru*
who	*er, eru*
wealth	*fjár*

Word List (English to Old Norse)

English	Old Norse	English	Old Norse
willing	fúss, fyrir		
went	ganga, Geitisson, gekk	**Y, y**	
walked	gengit		
weeping-for-joy	grátfeginn	you	mér, misjafnt, mögr, mun, mun, mun, mundi, mundu
wept	grét		
way	hátt, hefna, heiti, heitinn	yourself	sjálfr
was-named	hét	yours	sú, sumar, sumarit, svá, svá, svá, svarar, sverð, Svíðingi, synjat
where	hvaðan, hvar		
whether	hvárt, hvárt		
what	hverja, hverjum	your	þíns, þíns, þit
with	í, iðju, íþróttamaðr, klengisök, konu, kvað		
wife	konu		
would	mun, mundi, mundu, muni, munir		
will	munu, munum, næða, næst, næst		
word	orð, orð		
words	orð, orða, orðit		
worded	ortir		
we	oss, óvinum, óvizku		
wished	skyldi, skyldim		
wounded	stungizt		
why	því		
wood	tré		
would-be	væra, væri		
woke	vakti		
warned	varaðist		
were-you	varðtú		
witness	vátta		
witnesses	váttar, váttnefna		
well	vel		
worth	verðr, verr, verri		
worse	verr		
worsen	verri		
west	vestr		
winter	vetrinn		
widely	víða		
willed	vilda, vildi, vildi, vili		
wills	vildi		
wish	vilja		
wishes	vill		
wind	vindr		
wise	vitrir		

The Tale of Ale-Hood (*Old Icelandic*)

Old Icelandic	Literal	English
1	**1**	**1**
Þórhallur hét maður.	Thorhall was-named a-man.	There was a man named Thorhall.
Hann bjó í Bláskógum á Þórhallsstöðum.	He lived in Blawoods in Thorhallsstead.	He lived in Blawoods in Thorhallsstead.
Hann var vel fjáreigandi og heldur við aldur er saga sjá gerðist.	He was well property-owning and rather with age as story so happened.	He was a wealthy man and rather old when the story happened.
Lítill var hann og ljótur.	Small was he and ugly.	He was small and ugly.
Engi var hann íþróttamaður en þó var hann hagur við járn og tré.	None was he sports-man but though was he handy with iron and wood.	He was not a sporty man but he was handy with iron and wood.
Hann hafði þá iðju að gera öl á þingum til fjár sér	He had then occupation to make ale at assembly for wealth his	He had a job making ale at the assembly to earn money
en af þessi iðn varð hann brátt málkunnigur öllu stórmenni því að þeir keyptu mest mungát.	and of this craft became he soon talking-known all great-men because that they bought most ale.	and through this he came to talk to and get to know all the important people because they bought the most ale.
Var þá sem oft kann verða að mungátin eru misjafnt vinsæl og svo þeir er seldu.	Was then so often known was that ale was uneven-in popularity and so they who sold.	As often happens, not everyone liked the ale, or the man who sold it.
Engi var Þórhalldur veifiskati kallaður og heldur sínkur.	None was Thorhall spendthrift called and rather stingy.	Thorhall was no spendthrift, and people said he was rather stingy.
Honum voru augu þung.	His were eyes heavy.	His eyesight was poor.
Oftlega var það siður hans að hafa kofra á höfði og jafnan á þingum	Often was it custom him to have hood on head and equally at assembly	Often it was his habit to wear a hood, particularly at the assembly,

The Tale of Ale-Hood (Old Icelandic)

Old Icelandic	Literal	English
en af því að hann var maður ekki nafndrægur þá gáfu þingmenn honum það nafn er við hann festist að þeir kölluðu hann Ölkofra.	about of since that he was man not named then gave assemblymen him the name that with him fastened that they called him Ale-Hood.	and since people could not remember his name, they assembly people nickhamed him Ale-Hood, and the name stuck.
Það varð til tíðinda eitt haust að Ölkofri fór í skóg þann er hann átti og ætlaði að brenna kol sem hann gerði.	It was to news one autumn that Ale-Hood travelled to forest that which he had and intended to burn coal which he made.	And so it was one autumn that Ale-Hood travelled to the woods where he intended to make charcoal.
Skógur sá var upp frá Hrafnabjörgum og austur frá Lönguhlíð.	Forest so was up from Hrafnabjorg and east from Langahlid.	The wood was north of Hrafnabjorg and east of Langahlid.
Hann dvaldist þar nokkura daga og gerði til kola og brenndi síðan viðinn og vakti um nótt yfir gröfunum.	He dwelled there some days and made to coal and burned since trees and woke over night over pit.	He stayed there several days and made coal and then prepared the logs and kept watch over the pit.
En er leið á nóttina þá sofnaði hann	When was during the night then slept he	That was during the night, but then he fell asleep
en eldur kom upp í gröfunum og hljóp í limið hjá og logaði það brátt.	but fire came up in pit and ran to foliage beside and blazed that soon.	and fire flared up in the pit and caught the branches and they were ablaze.
Því næst hljóp eldur í skóginn.	Then next ran fire to forest.	Then the fire ran through the next wood.
Tók hann þá að brenna.	Took it then to burn.	It then began to burn.
Þá gerist á vindur hvass.	Then was the wind sharp.	Then a sharp wind blew.
Nú vaknaði Ölkofri og varð því feginn að hann gæti sér forðað.	Now awoke Ale-Hood and was then relieved that he got himself avoided.	Now Ale-Hood awoke and thought he was lucky to have avoided the fire.
Eldurinn hljóp í skóginn.	Fire ran among forest.	The fire ran through the woods.
Brann sá skógur fyrst allur er Ölkofri átti en síðan hljóp eldur í þá skóga er þar voru næstir og brunnu skógar víða um hraunið.	Burnt so forest first all that Ale-Hood had then afterwards ran fire to then forest that there was nearest and burned forests widely about lava-fields.	Burnt first were the woods that Ale-Hood owned, then the next woods, then afterwards the fire ran to the woods around the lava fields.

The Tale of Ale-Hood (Old Icelandic)

Old Icelandic	Literal	English
Er þar nú kallað á Sviðningi.	That there now called is Svidning.	There it is now called Svidning.
Þar brann skógur sá er kallaður var Goðaskógur.	There burned forest that then called was Godaskogur.	There the wood was burned that was called Goda Wood.
Hann áttu sex goðar.	It had six chieftans.	It belonged to six chieftains.
Einn var Snorri goði, annar Guðmundur Eyjólfsson, þriðji Skafti lögmaður, fjórði Þorkell Geitisson, fimmti Eyjólfur son Þórðar gellis, sétti Þorkell trefill Rauða-Bjarnarson.	One was Snorri chieftan, another Gudmund Son-of-Eyjolf, third Skafti law-speaker, fourth Thorkell Son-of-Geiti, fifth Eyjolf son Thord gellir, sixth Thorkell trefill Son-of-Rauda-Bjarn.	One chieftan was Snorri the Priest, another Gudmund Eyjolfson, Skafti the Lawspeaker, Thorkel Geitisson, Eyjolf son of Thord Gellir, and sixth Thorkell Trefill son of Red-Bear.
Þeir höfðu keypt skóga þá til þess að hafa til nytja sér á þingi.	They had bought forest then to this to have to use themselves at assembly.	They had bought the wood for their own use at the assembly.
Eftir kolbrennu þessa fór Ölkofri heim.	After coal-burning this travelled Ale-Hood home.	After this coal burning Ale-Hood travelled home.
En tíðindi þessi spurðust víða um héruð og komu fyrst til Skafta þeirra mann er fyrir sköðum höfðu orðið.	About news this asked many about district and came first to Skafti of-the men who for damage had word.	News about this was learned around the district and came to Skafti, the first of the six men whose woods had been damaged had word.
Um haustið sendi hann orð norður til Eyjafjarðar með þeim mönnum er ferð áttu milli héraða og lét segja Guðmundi skógabrennuna og það með að það mál var févænlegt.	Around autumn sent he word north to Eyjafjord with those men who travelled directions between districts and let said Gudmund forest-burning and with it that the matter was money-promising.	Around autumn he sent word north to Eyafjord with men who travelled between districts and told Gudmund about the wood burning and with it that the matter could be profitable.
Slík erindi fóru og vestur í héruð til þeirra manna er skóga höfðu átt.	Such errand travelled and west to districts to those men who forest had owned.	Such errands were travelled to the west, to the districts where the other owners were.
Fóru þá sendiboð um veturinn eftir milli þeirra allra og það með að goðar þeir sex skyldu hittast á þingi og vera allir að einu ráði	Travelled then messenger about winter after between they all and to among the chieftans they six should meet at assembly and be all as one counsel	Messengers travelled through the winter between all six chieftains that they should meet at the assembly and take joint action
en Skafti skyldi mál til búa því að hann sat næst.	as Skafti wished matter to settle since that he sat nearest.	and Skafti would start the matter since he lived nearest.

The Tale of Ale-Hood (Old Icelandic)

Old Icelandic	Literal	English
En er vor kom og stefnudagar þá reið Skafti til með marga menn og stefndi Ölkofra um skógabrennuna og lét varða skóggang.	In the spring came and policy-days then rode Skafti to with many men and summons Ale-Hood about forest-burning and let concerning outlawry.	In the spring, at summons days, Skafti then rode with many men and summoned Ale-Hood for the burning of the wood under threat of outlawry.
Ölkofri var málóði og heldur stórorðu, lét þess von ef vinir hans kæmu til þings að Skafti mundi eigi jafnstórlega láta.	Ale-Hood was of-strong-language and rather high-sounding, let this wished if friends his came to assembly that Skafti would not equally-great leave.	Ale-Hood was swearing and shouting, and said that if his friends came to the assembly that Skafti would not be equally great.
Skafti svaraði fá og reið á brott.	Skafti answered few and rode to away.	Skafti answered little and rode away.
Um sumarið eftir komu goðar þeir sex til þings er skóga höfðu átt og höfðu brátt stefnu sín á milli og var það ráðið að mál skyldi fram hafa en gera fé allmikið ella hafa sjálfdæmi.	About summer after came chieftans they six to assembly who forest owned had and had soon summons they about between and was it decided the matter should from-forward have as made fee all-much otherwise have self-judgement.	In the summer the six chieftains who owned the woods came to the assembly and talked between themselves about the summons, and it was decided that the matter should be heavy damages if they could not have self-judgement.
Ölkofri kom til þings og átti mungát að selja,	Ale-Hood came to assembly and had ale to sell,	Ale-Hood came to the assembly and had ale to sell,
kom þá til fundar við vini sína þá sem vanir voru að kaupa öl að honum.	came then to meet with friends his then as friends were to buy ale of him.	coming to meet with his friends who bought ale from him.
Hann bað þá liðs og bauð þeim öl að selja	He invited then people and offered them ale to sell	He invited people and offered to sell them ale
en þeir svöruðu allir á einn veg að þau ein kaup hefðu þeir við ást að þeim var ekki vilnað í, sögðu að þeir mundu eigi þeim birni beitast að deila um mál hans við ofureflismenn slíka og vildi engi maður heita honum liði og engi vildi eiga kaup við hann.	but they answered all the one way that they only bought had they with affection that they were not willed to, said that they would not they bear employing to share about the-matter his with ultra-strong-men such and willed no man call him help and none willed have buy with him.	but they all answered the same way, that they had not bought out of affection, and that they were not obliged to him, and they would not seek to get involved in his matter, especially since they were such powerful men, and no one wanted to help or even buy any of his ale.

The Tale of Ale-Hood (Old Icelandic)

Old Icelandic	Literal	English
Þótti honum þá heldur vandast málið.	Seemed to-him then rather difficult matter.	It looked to him that the situation was becoming rather tricky.
Gekk hann þá milli búða og fékk þá engi andsvör þótt hann bæði menn liðs.	Went he then between booths and got then no answers though he asked people help.	He then went among the booths and got no answers to his asking for help.
Var þá lokið stórleika hans og drambi.	Was then ended pride his and arrogance.	He did not have any pride or arrogance left.
Það var um dag einn að Ölkofri kom til búðar Þorsteins Síðu-Hallssonar og fekk fyrir hann og bað sér liðs.	That was about day one that Ale-Hood came to booth Thorstein Son-of-Sidu-Hall and got before him and asked his help.	It was one day that Ale-Hood came to the booth of Thorstein Hallsson and came before him and asked for his help.
Þorsteinn veitti honum slík andsvör sem aðrir.	Thorstein granted him such answer as others.	Thorstein gave him the same answer as the others.

2

Old Icelandic	Literal	English
Maður er nefndur Broddi Bjarnason, mágur Þorsteins.	Man was named Broddi Bjarnason, brother-in-law Thorstein's.	There was a man camed Broddi Bjarnarson, Thorstein's brother-in-law.
Hann sat hið næsta honum.	He sat then next-to him.	He was sitting next to him.
Broddi var þá á tvítugsaldri.	Broddi was then about twenty-aged.	Broddi was then aged about twenty.
Ölkofri gekk út með búðinni þá er Þorsteinn hafði synjað honum liðs.	Ale-Hood went out-of among booths then as Thorstein had refused him help.	Ale-Hood went out of the booth as Thorstein had refused to help him.
Broddi mælti þá:	Broddi said then:	Broddi then said:
"Svo líst mér mágur sem þessi maður muni ekki vel til skógarmanns felldur og er það lítilræði að sekja hann þeim er miklir þykjast fyrir sér.	"So like to-me brother-in-law that this man should not well to outlawry fall and was it little-advised that seek him they that great consider therefore themselves.	"It seems to be brother-in-law that this man should not be an outlaw and it was mean-spirited that they seek this for him, those who consider themselves so important.
Nú er það drengskapur mágur að veita honum lið og mun þér það sýnast ráð".	Now is that word-of-honour brother-in-law that grant him help and should you that appear counsel".	Now it would be honourable, brother-in-law, that we give him help and you appear as counsel".

The Tale of Ale-Hood (Old Icelandic)

Old Icelandic	Literal	English
Þorsteinn svarar:	Thorstein answered:	Thorstein answered:
"Veittu honum lið ef þú ert allfús til en veita mun eg þér brautargengi til þess sem annars".	"Grant him assistance if you are all-happy to and grant should i to-you path-assistance to this as others".	"Give him help if you are happy to, and I shall give you assistance on this path as I do others".
Broddi mælti við mann einn að ganga skyldi eftir Ölkofra.	Broddi spoke with man one that go should after Ale-Hood.	Broddi spoke with a man and asked him to go after Ale-Hood.
Sá gerði svo, gekk út og þar hjá búðarvegginum hitti hann Ölkofra.	So done so, went out and there beside booth-walls found he Ale-Hood.	So it was done, he went out and there beside the booth walls he found Ale-Hood.
Stóð hann þar og grét aumlega.	Stood he there and wept abjectly.	He was stood there weeping abjectly.
Þessi maður bað hann ganga inn í búðina og taka af sér ópið "og eigi skaltu snökta er þú kemur til Þorsteins".	This man invited him to-go in to booth and take of him open "and not shall-you sob as you come to Thorstein".	The man invited him to go into the booth and stop himself shrieking "and don't be sobbing when you come to Thorstein".
Ölkofri varð grátfeginn og gerði svo.	Ale-Hood became weeping-for-joy and did so.	Ale-Hood started weeping with joy and did so.
En er þeir komu fyrir Þorstein þá tók Broddi til orða:	Then as they came before Thorstein then took Broddi to words:	Then as they came before Thorstein then Broddi started to speak:
"Svo þykir mér sem Þorsteinn vilji þér lið veita og þykir honum þetta klengisök vera.	"So seems to me Thorstein willing to-you assistance know and seems to-him that small-blame be.	"So it seems to me Thorstein is willing to help you, and it seems to him that there is small blame.
Máttir þú eigi gæta skóga þeirra er þú brenndir þann er þú áttir".	May you not guarded forest theirs when you burned then that you had".	You may not have been able to guard against their woods burning when your own had burned down.
Ölkofri mætli:	Ale-Hood said:	Ale-Hood said:
"Hver er sjá hinn sæli maður er nú mælir við mig?" "Broddi heiti ég", segir hann.	"Who is this the good man that now speaks with me?" "Broddi named i", said he.	"Who is this good man that now speaks with me?"
"Hver er sjá hinn sæli maður er nú mælir við mig?" "Broddi heiti ég", segir hann.	"Who is this the good man that now speaks with me?" "Broddi named i", said he.	"I am named Broddi", he said.

The Tale of Ale-Hood (Old Icelandic)

Old Icelandic	Literal	English
Þá mælti Ölkofri:	Then spoke Ale-Hood:	Then Ale-Hood spoke:
"Hvert er hér Broddi Bjarnason?"	"Which is here Broddi Bjarnason?"	"He who is named Broddi Bjarnarson?"
"Svo er", segir Broddi.	"So is", said Broddi.	"So it is", said Broddi.
"Bæði er", kvað Ölkofri, "að þú ert göfulegri að sjá en aðrir menn enda áttu til þess varið",	"Both are", said Ale-Hood, "that you are nobler to this than other people in-the-end have to this defend",	"Both are", said Ale-Hood, "that you are nobler to see than other men, in-the-end to your family's worth",
for hann þar mörgum orðum um og gerist þá hraustur í máli.	for he there many words about and was then brave to speak.	and he went on to speak many words about it and became braver.
"Hitt er nú til", kvað Þorsteinn, "ef þú ert allfús til Broddi að veita honum nokkuð lið er þó lofar hann þig svo mjög".	"Find i now to", said Thorstein, "if you are all-happy to Broddi to grant him some assistance as though praises he you so much".	"Now I find towards", said Thorstein, "if you are happy to give him some assistance since he praises you so much".
Broddi stóð þá upp og mart manna með honum.	Broddi stood then up and many men with him.	Broddi then stood up, and with many many with him.
Gekk hann út úr búðinni.	Went he from out-of booth.	He went out of his booth.
Hann brá þá Ölkofra á einmæli og ræddi við hann.	He drew then Ale-Hood to one-talk and discussed with him.	He then took Ale-Hood to talk privately and discuss with him.
Síðan ganga þeir upp á völluna.	Afterwards went they up to plains.	Afterwards they went up to the assembly plains.
Var þar fyrir mart manna.	Were there before many men.	There were many men before them.
Höfðu þeir þá verið í lögréttu.	Had they then been at law-assembly.	They had been at the law-assembly.
En er aðrir menn höfðu í brott gengið þá sátu þeir eftir Guðmundur og Skafti og ræddu um lög.	And as other men had to away walked then sat they behind Gudmund and Skafti and discussed about law.	As the other men left, there sat behind Gudmund and Skafti discussing law.

The Tale of Ale-Hood (Old Icelandic)

Old Icelandic	Literal	English
Broddi og förunautar hans reikuðu um völluna en Ölkofri gekk í lögréttuna.	Broddi and companions his roamed about plains but Ale-Hood went to law-assembly.	Broddi and his companions walked about the assembly plains but Ale-Hood went to the law-assembly.
Hann féll til jarðar allur og kraup til fóta með þeim og mælti:	He fell to earth all and kneeled about feet among them and said:	He fell to the ground and kneeled at their feet among them and said:
"Sæll er eg orðinn er eg hefi ykkur fundið hina dýrlegu menn og höfðingja mína eða munuð þið nokkuð vilja mér hjálpa hinir góðu menn þót eg sé ómaklegur því að eg verð nú allur fyrir borði nema þið dugið mér?"	"Happy am i become that i have you found then dearly men and chieftans mine but shall you some wish to-me help other good men though i so uncomfortable because that i deserve not all before borne take you enough of-me?"	"I am happy to have found you my dear men and chieftains, but should some of you wish to help me, good people, though I do not deserve it, I am uncomfortable because now I will be all before the table unless enough of you are with me?"
Seint er að telja öll orð Ölkofra þau er hann mælti og lét hann ssem aumlegast á allan hátt.	Late is to tell all words Ale-hood's his that he spoke and let him as miserable in every way.	It would take too long to tell all of Ale-Hood's words that he spoke as he was miserable in every way.
Þá mætli Guðmundur til Skafta:	Then said Gudmund to Skafti:	Then Gudmund said to Skafti:
"Allvesallega lætur þessi maður".	"Miserable behaviour this man".	"What miserable behaviour from this man".
Skafti svarar:	Skafti answered:	Skafti answered:
"Hvar er nú Ölkofri stórlæti þitt? Ólíklegt þótti þér í vor þá er vér fórum stefnuför að sá mundi þinn hinn besti kostur að leggja málið undir mig eða hversu drjúgir verða þeir þér nú í liðveilsunni höfðingjarnir er þú hættir mér í vor?"	"Where is now Ale-Hood pride yours Unlike seem you as spring then as we travelled summons to-you so could you the best choice to allow the-matter under me but how substantial were they to-you now the supportive chieftans that you mannered to-me about spring?"	"Where is your pride now Ale-Hood? You seem different from the spring when we travelled to summon you, so you could make the best choice to have the matter judged by me, but how substantial have you found the supportive chieftains that you threatened me with in the spring?"
Ölkofri segir:	Ale-Hood said:	Ale-Hood said:

The Tale of Ale-Hood (Old Icelandic)

Old Icelandic	Literal	English
"Ær var eg þá og þó verr er eg vildi það eigi að þú dæmdir um mitt mál enda gettu eigi höfðingja því að þeir eru örhjarta allir þegar þeir sjá ykkur að koma.	"Awed was i then and though worse am i willed it not to you deem about my matter in-the-end getting no chieftans because that they were un-heartened all as-soon-as they saw you that came.	"I was awed then, and worse that I willed it not to be judged by you in the matter, getting no chieftains in the end because they were disheartened as soon as they saw that you had come.
Sæll væri eg þá ef eg næði því að koma undir ykkur mínu máli.	Happy would-be i then if i neared therefore to come under you my matter.	How happy I would be if I could be nearer to my matter coming under you.
Eða á eg nokkura von þess? En vorkunn er það Skafti minn að þú hafir mér svo reiðst að nú sé þess engi kostur.	But to i some hope this Then pity i that Skafti mine that you have to-me such counsel that now see this none choice.	But what hope is there of this? Then it is a pity that you have given me such counsel that I now see this is not a choice.
Var eg þá fól og afglapi er eg neitaði gerð þinni	Was i then fool and simpleton that i refusal made yours	I was then a fool and a simpleton to refuse your offer
en eg þori eigi að sjá þá grimmu menn er þegar munu drepa mig ef þið hjálpið mér eigi við".	that i greater-part not to saw then grim men that straight-away will kill me if you help me not with".	that I saw no greater part then, the terrible men that will kill me straight away if you do not help me with this".
Hann mælti oft hið sama, sagði svo að hann þóttist sæll ef þeir skyldu dæma hans mál:	He spoke often the same, said so that he thought happy if they should deem his matter:	He often said the same things, saying that he thought he would be happy if they should judge the matter.
"Þykir mér það mitt fé best komið er þið hafið".	"Think i that my money best comes that you have".	"I think that my money would be best if you have it".
Guðmundur mælti til Skafta:	Gudmund said to Skafti:	Gudmund spoke to Skafti:
"Ekki ætla eg þenna vel til sektar fallinn eða mun eigi hitt heldur ráð að við gerum hann feginn og látum hann kjósa menn til gerðar þessar?	"Not intend i that well to guilt fall but should not find rather advice to with being he relieved and let he choose people to do this	"I don't suppose it will be well if he falls guilty, and should it not rather be the decision left with him to choose people to do this? Though I know not how others alike is this matter agreed with him".
Þó veit eg eigi hversu hinum líkar er þetta mál eiga við hann".	Though know i not how-so others alike is this matter said-of with him".	Though I don't know how others are alike in this matter being agreed with him".

The Tale of Ale-Hood (Old Icelandic)

Old Icelandic	Literal	English
"Nú þá hinir góðu menn", segir Ölkofri, "veitið mér þá nokkurn dugnað eftir".	"Now then other good men", said Ale-Hood, "know i then someone assistance after".	"Now then other good men", said Ale-Hood, "I know then that you will give me some assistance after".
Skafti mælti:	Skafti said:	Skafti said:
"Undir mér er lykt máls þessa því að eg fer með sökina.	"Under me is conclusion matter this therefore that i go with seeking.	"Under me is the judgement of this matter, therefore I will seek to resolve it.
Munum við til þess hætta Ölkofri að við Guðmundur gerum um og lúkum málinu.	Should on to this end Ale-Hood that with Gudmund be about and conclude case.	So to that end, Ale-Hood, the case will be concluded with Gudmund.
Get eg að þér muni það duga við fullting okkart".	Get i that you would that help with assistance ours".	That is how it would help you with our assistance".
Þá stóð Ölkofri upp og takast þeir síðan í hendur.	Then stood Ale-Hood up and took them then in hand.	Then Ale-Hood stood up and took them then in hand.
Nefndi Ölkofri þegar votta hvern að öðrum og er vottnefna kom upp þá drifu menn að.	Named Ale-Hood then witness each to others and as witnesses came up then flocked many to.	Ale-Hood then named each of his witnesses, and many people crowded around.
Nefndi Ölkofri fyrst Brodda og förunauta hans.	Named Ale-Hood first Brodda and companions his.	Ale-Hood named Broddi and his companions.
Skafti mælti:	Skafti spoke:	Skafti spoke:
"Sökunautur vor biður okkur Guðmund til gerðar um mál þetta en þó að vér höfum það staðfest með oss er skaða höfum fengið að sjálfdæmi skyldi fyrir koma þá viljum við Guðmundur það nú veita honum að við gerum heldur um en aðrir ef Þórhallur vill það kjörið hafa.	"Defendant our invited us Gudmund to do about matter this and though that we have that confirmed with us that damages have got to self-judgement should by coming then will we Gudmund that now provide him to with doing rather of the others if Thorhall wishes that choice have.	"The defendant has invited Gudmund and myself to do about this matter, and though we have confirmed that those who suffered the loss are to accept self-judgement, Gudmund and I are willing to grant Ale-Hood this much, that we two rather than any other men shall decide the matter if Thorhall agrees.
Skuluð þér þess nefndir vottar að fyrir mál þetta skal fé gera en eigi mannsektir.	Should you this name witnesses as for the-matter that shall money make about only fines.	You should stand witness for the matter that only damages shall be awarded.

The Tale of Ale-Hood (Old Icelandic)

Old Icelandic	Literal	English
Eg handsala niðurfall að sökum þeim er eg stefndi í vor".	I confirm dropping the blame those that i summonsed in spring".	I confirm that I drop the charge for which I summoned him in the spring.
Síðan slitu þeir handlaginu.	After dissolved they handshake.	Then they dissolved with a handshake.
Þá mælti Skafti við Guðmund:	Then spoke Skafti with Gudmund:	Then Skafti spoke with Gudmund.
"Hví mun eigi vel að við lúkum þessu af?"	"Why should not well that we conclude this of?"	"Why don't we conclude this?"
"Vel má það", segir Guðmundur.	"Well may that", said Gudmund.	"That may well be", said Gudmund.
Ölkofri mælti:	Ale-Hood spoke:	Ale-Hood spoke:
"Ekki skuluð þið hrapa því svo því að eg er ekki ráðinn í að kjósa ykkur heldur en aðra menn".	"Not should you hurry therefore so for that i am not decided of to choose you rather than other people".	"You should not be in such a hurry, because I have not decided if I choose you or rather someone else".
Guðmundur mælti:	Gudmund spoke:	Gudmund spoke:
"Svo var skilt að við skyldum gera nema þú kjörir heldur þá aðra er þetta mál eiga með okkur".	"So was divided that we should do taking your choice rather then others that this matter have with us".	"It was so agreed that Skafti and I would decide rather than others who would have this matter with us".
Ölkofri segir:	Ale-Hood said:	Ale-Hood said:
"Því neitaði eg allan tíma að þeir skyldu gera en svo var skilið í handlagi að eg skyldi kjósa tvo menn til þá er eg vildi".	"Since refused i all time that they should do about so was divided at agreement that i should choose two men for then as i willed".	"I never agreed at the time that these men should decide, it was agreed at the handshake that I could choose any two men I wanted".
Þá var leitað um handsalsvætti	Then was sought about agreement	Then the agreement was sought about the assembly,

The Tale of Ale-Hood (Old Icelandic)

Old Icelandic	Literal	English
en þingmenn Guðmundar og Skafta deildust allmjög að hversu skilið var en Broddi og förunautar hans skáru skýrt úr að svo hafði skilið verið sem Ölkofri sagði að hann skyldi kjósa menn til gerðar.	the assembly Gudmund and Skafti judged all-greatly that how understood was that Broddi and companions his cut clear of that so had understood been which Ale-Hood said that he should choose man to do.	Then the agreement was sought about the assembly, Gudmund and Skafti disagreed greatly about how it had been agreed, but Broddi and his companions were clear about how it was understood, as Ale-Hood had said, that he could choose the men to decide.
Þá mælti Skafti:	Then spoke Skafti:	Then Skafti Spoke:
"Hvaðan rann sjá alda undir Ölkofri? Sé eg að þú heldur nokkuru rakkara halanum en fyrir stundu áðan	"Where runs this wave from-beneath Ale-Hood See i that you rather somewhat bolder tail-wagging than before awhile earlier	"Where runs this wave from beneath you Ale-Hood? I see that you are wagging your tail more boldy than before,
eða hverja menn muntu kjósa til gerðar?"	but what men should choose to do?"	and which men do you choose to decide?
Ölkofri mælti:	Ale-Hood spoke:	Ale-Hood spoke:
"Ekki skal lengi að því hyggja.	"Not shall longer to for think.	"I shall think on it no longer.
Eg kýs Þorstein Hallsson og Brodda Bjarnason mág hans og ætla eg að þá sé málið beutr komið en þið gerið um".	I choose Thorstein Hallsson and Brodda Bjarnason brother-in-law his and intend i that then so matter better comes than you make about".	I choose Thorstein Hallsson and his brother-in-law Broddi Bjarnarson, and I suppose that the matter will be better than if undertaken by you".
Skafti sagði að hann ætlaði að það mál væri vel komið þótt þeir gerðu um	Skafti said to him intended that this matter would-be well coming though they made about	Skafti said to him that he supposed that this matter would be in good hands if they undertook it.
því að málaefni voru eru brýn og góð en þeir eru svo vitrir að þeir munu sjá kunna hversu þungs þú ert af verður.	as the matters are they urgent and good and they are so wise that they should this know how-so heavily you are of worth.	"As the case is urgent and just and they are wise men, they should know how heavily you shall be dealt with".
Ölkofri gekk þá í lið Brodda og fóru menn heim til búða.	Ale-Hood went then with company Brodda's and travelled men home to booths.	Ale-Hood went then with Brodda's company and the men travelled home to their booths.

The Tale of Ale-Hood (Old Icelandic)

Old Icelandic	Literal	English
3	3	3
Eftir um daginn skyldi upp segja sætt.	Later in the-day should up said settlement.	Later in the day the verdict was to be announced.
Báru þeir þá ráð sín saman Þorsteinn og Broddi.	Bore they then matter theirs together Thorstein and Broddi.	Thorstein and Broddi started to consider the matter.
Vildi Þorsteinn meira gera en Broddi kvað það skýrst að gera svo sem hann vildi og segja þá sjálfur sátt upp.	Willed Thorstein more to-do than Broddi said it clarified to be so as he willed and say then himself settlement up.	Thorstein wanted more of a settlement than Broddi did, and it was agreed that it would be as he said.
Broddi bað hann kjósa hvort er hann vildi,	Broddi asked him choose either as he willed,	Broddi invited him to choose either as he wished,
segja sátt upp eða sitja fyrir svörum ef nokkurir menn yrðu til að leiða á gerðina.	say settlement up or sit before answers if some men be to the objection to make.	to decide the settlement or sit in judgement and answer any objections.
Þorsteinn lést heldur vilja segja sátt upp en skipta hnæfilyrðum við þá goðana.	Thorstein let rather willed say settlement up than exchange blows with then chieftans.	Thorstein said that he would rather give the judgement than exchange blows with the chieftains.
Síðan sagði Þorsteinn að Ölkofri skyldi eigi lengi þurfa síns hluta að bíða, kvað þá skyldu gjaldast féið allt að Lögbergi.	Since said Thorstein that Ale-Hood should not long need his lot to wait, said then should pay fee altogether at Law-Rock.	Then Thorstein said that Ale-Hood would not need to wait long, saying that then the payment of a fee should be made altogether at the law rock.
Síðan gengu þeir til Lögbergs.	Then went they to Law-Rock.	Then they went to the law rock.
En er lokið var þar lögskil að mæla þá spurði Þorsteinn Hallsson hvort goðar þeir væru að Lögbergi er mál áttu að kæra við Ölkofra:	And when ended were there legal-settlement to matters then asked Thorstein Hallsson whether chieftans they were at Law-Rock that matter had to accuse with Ale-Hood:	And when the other legal settlements were done, Thorstein Halsson asked whether the chieftains who had brought the accusation against Ale-Hood were present:
"Mér er svo sagt að við Broddi skulum gera um mál það.	"To-me is so said that with Broddi should make about matter that.	"It has been said to me that Broddi and I shall settle the matter.
Munum við nú upp lúka gerðinni ef þér viljið til hlýða".	Should with now up finish make if you will to listen".	We shall deliver the conclusion if you are ready to listen".

The Tale of Ale-Hood (Old Icelandic)

Old Icelandic	Literal	English
Þeir sögðust góðs að vænta að þeir mundu réttlátir í gerðinni.	They said good to expect that they would right-like to make.	They said they expected the decision would be just.
Þá mælti Þorsteinn:	Then spoke Thorstein:	Then Thorstein spoke:
"Svo líst okkur á sem lítils sé fyrir vert um skóga yðra félaga.	"So beholding ours is that little being for worth about forest yours companions.	"So is our finding that your wood and that of your companions is of little worth.
Voru þeir félitlir og fjárlægir yður itl gagns.	Were they fee-little and financial yours little benefit.	They were worth very little financially for you to benefit.
Var eigngirni mikil í þeim mönnum er góðs áttu kost og kalla það meigu sinni annarri	Was selfish great that these men the chieftans had benefit and call that may opinion another	It was a great selfishness that these chieftains had benefitted from this property in this way,
en hann mátti eigi ábyrgjast yðvarn skóg er hann brenndi sinn skóg og eru slíkt voðaverk.	that he may not guarantee your forest that he burned his forest and are such accidents.	and another opinion is that he could not have guaranteed to save your woods once his had burned, and it is therefore as such an accident.
En fyrir því að það er í gerð lagt þá skal gera nokkuð fyrir.	But for because that it is to made laid then shall be-done something for.	But because this settlement is to be made then something shall be done.
Þér sex menn hafið átt skógana.	Then six men have had forests.	These six men who own the woods.
Nú viljum vér gera sex alnar hverjum yðrum og skal það gjaldast hér þegar".	Now will we make six measures each yours and shall that be-paid here straightaway".	Now we will award six measures, one for each of you that shall be paid here immediately".
Broddi hafði búist og stikað vaðmál í sundur og kastar hann þá sér hverjum stúf til þeirra og mælti:	Broddi had prepared and stitched homespun-cloth to asunder and cast he then theirs each stump to them and said:	Broddi had prepared and stitched a homespun cloth and cast each strip down to them and said:
"Slíkt kalla eg argaskatt".	"Such call i cowardly".	I call this a tribute to the dastardly.
Skafti segir:	Skafti said:	Skafti said:
"Auðsætt er það Broddi að þú ert fús til að eiga illt við oss.	"Obvious is it Broddi that you are willing to that have ill with us.	"It is obvious Broddi that you wish to have bad will with us.

The Tale of Ale-Hood (Old Icelandic)

Old Icelandic	Literal	English
Hefir þú mjög stungist til þessa máls og ferð þú lítt þverafæti að fjandskap við oss.	Have you much wounded about this matter and go you little foot-around to fiend-ship with us.	You have made a great wound in this matter, and you do not tip-toe around making enemies of us.
Kann vera að oss falli önnur mál lettara".	Can be that ours fall another matter easier".	It can be that other law suits will be resolved more easily".
Broddi svarar:	Broddi answered:	Broddi answered:
"Þurfa muntu þess Skafti að taka meira á öðrum sakferlum ef skríða skal í það skarð er Ormur frændi þinn reytti af þér fyrir mansöngsdrápu er þú ortir um konu hans.	"Need should this Skafti to take more of other lawsuits if action shall to that gap that Orm kinsmen yours tried of you for love-song-poem that you worded about wife his.	You need to make more money from other law suits, Skafti, to make up for the damages your kinsman Orm got from you for the love-poem you composed about his wife.
Var það illa gert enda var það illa goldið"	Was that ill done in-the-end was that ill paid?"	Was that bad will all paid in the end?"
Þá mælti Þorkell trefill:	Then spoke Thorkell trefill:	Then Thorkell Trefill spoke:
"Allmjög missýnist slíkum manni sem Broddi er.	"All-much mistake such man as Broddi that.	"That was very much a mistake from such a man as Broddi.
Hann vill hafa vináttu Ölkofra eða nokkurar mútugjafir og kaupa svo að gera sér að óvinum slíka menn sem hann hefir í fangi".	He will have friendship Ale-hood's or some bribes and bought so that made his to un-friends such men as he has to enemies".	That he will have Ale-Hood's friendship, or his bribes, so that he makes his opponents into enemies".
Broddi segir:	Broddi said:	Broddi said:
"Ekki er það missýni að halda einurð sinni þótt mannamunur sé með yður Ölkofra.	"Not is that mistake to hold determined his thought integrity as with yours Ale-Hood.	"It is no mistake to hold with determination to your integrity, yours or Ale-Hood's.

The Tale of Ale-Hood (Old Icelandic)

Old Icelandic	Literal	English
En hitt var glámsýni í vor er þú reiðst til vorþings að þú varaðist eigi það er Steingrímur hafði stóðhest selfeitan og lagðist hann upp að baki þér en merin sú er þú reiðst var mögur og féll hún undir þér og hefi eg eigi spurt til sanns hverjum þá slauðraði en hitt sáu menn að þú varst lengi fastur því að hesturinn lagði fæturna fram yfir kápuna".	But find then big-mistake in spring when you rode to local-assembly that you warned not-of it that Steingrim had stallion fat and laid he up to back you as mare yours were you riding was skinny and fell she under you also have i not asked about the-truth whether then trailing-behind about found this people that you were long fastened with the horse laid feet from across cloak".	But you yourself made a big mistake in the spring when you rode to a local assembly, you were not aware of the fat stallion that Steingrim had until he was laid up to your backside, and you were riding that skinny mare as she fell under you, and I have never learned the truth whether those trailing behind you found that you were long fastened with the horse with his feet laid across your cloak".
Eyjólfur Þórðarson mætli:	Eyjolf Thordarson spoke:	Eyjolf Thordarson spoke:
"Það er satt að segja að sjá maður hefur allmjög dregið burst úr nefi oss enda mælir rán og regin við oss á sogört ofan".	"It is true to say that this man has all-much drawn cheated from noses ours in-the-end talking robbery and ruling with us by saying over".	"It is true that this man has cheated us out of our reward in front of our noses, and heaping abuse over us".
Broddi segir:	Broddi said:	Broddi said:
"Eigi hefi eg dregið burst úr nefi yður.	"Not have i drawn cheated of noses yours.	"I have not cheated you of your noses.
Þá var dregin burst úr nefi þér er þú fórst norðu til Skagafjarðar og stalst öxnum frá Þorkeli Eiríkssyni en Guðdala-Starri reið eftir þér og sástu þá eftirförina er þér voruð komnir í Vatnsdal.	Then were drawn cheated of nose you as you travelled north to Skagafjord and stealing oxen from Thorkell Eriksson and Guddala-Starri rode after you and saw-you then after-travelling that you were coming to Vatnsdal.	You were cheated of your nose as you travelled north to Skagafjord stealing oxen from Thorkell Eriksson and Guddala-Starri rode after you, and then you reached Vatnsdal.
Varðstu þá svo hræddur að þú brást þér í merarlíki og voru slíkt firn mikil en þeir Starri ráku aftur öxnina og var það satt að hann dró burst úr nefi þér".	Were-you then so scared that you transformed you to mare-like and were so awful much that they Starri drove back oxen and was that true that he drew cheated of nose you".	You were so scared that you turned yourself into a mare, an awful thing to do, and Starri drove the oxen back, so it is true, he cheated your nose".
Þá mælti Snorri goði:	Then spoke Snorri chieftan:	Then Snorri the chieftain spoke:

The Tale of Ale-Hood (Old Icelandic)

Old Icelandic	Literal	English
"Allt er oss annað tiltækilegra en deila hér illyrðum við Brodda en það er líkast að vér gerum oss minnisamt um fjandskap þenna er Broddi lýsir við oss ef vér komumst í færi".	"All are we other available than sharing here malice with Broddi but it is likely that we make us memorable about fiend-ship this that Broddi declared with us if we come to opportunity".	We would all rather be unavailable than here sharing malice with Broddi, but it is likely that we shall have it remembered what fiendship Broddi has shown us, and how it has come to be.
Broddi segir:	Broddi said:	Broddi said:
"Um snýrð þú þá sæmdunum Snorri ef þú leggur allan hug á að hefna mér en þú hefnir eigi föður þíns".	"Around turned you then honour Snorri if you lay all mind to that revenge to-me than you avenge not father yours".	"Your honour is turned around then, Snorri, if you put your mind to revenge that instead of avenging your father".
Þá mælti Þorkell Geitisson:	Then spoke Thorkell Geitisson:	Then Thorkell Geitisson spoke:
"Þetta er líkast að þú hafir það helst af nafni því er þú ert eftir heitinn að hann vildi hvers manns hlut óhæfan af sér verða láta og það annað að menn þoli eigi og liggir þú drepinn er stundir líða".	"It is likely that you have that held of the-name of that you are after named that he wills each man's lot trouble of himself being let and that other of men tolerate not and laying you killed be awhile passed".	It is likely, that all you have held of the name your father gave to you, is to make trouble with every man, other men will not tolerate it and you may be killed after a while.
Broddi segir:	Broddi said:	Broddi said:
"Engi vegur er okkur í frændi að yppa hér fyrir alþýðu ógæfu frænda vorra en ekki skal þess dylja er margir vita að Brodd-Helgi var veginn.	"No way is ours of kinsmen that up here before the-people un-giving kinsmen talking-loudly about not shall this disguise that many knowing that Brodd-Helgi was killed.	"There is no way to gain anything, kinsmen, by talking loudly, this shall not disguise that many know that Brodd-Helgi was killed.
Var mér og það sagt að faðir þinn tæki ofarlega til þeirra launanna en hitt ætla eg ef þú leitar að er þú munir fingrum kenn það er faðir minn markaði þig í Böðvarsdal".	Was i and that told that father yours took high-up to their loans but find suppose i if you seek that as you should fingers know that was father mine marked you in Bodvarsdale".	I was told that your father paid the highest price, but I suppose that if you find your fingers, then they will find where my father marked you at Bodvarsdale".
Eftir það skildust þeir og engu heim til búðar.	After that separated they and none home to booths.	After that they separated and went back home to their booths.
Er nú Ölkofri úr sögunni.	Is now Ale-Hood out-of the-saga.	Ale-Hood is now out of the saga.

The Tale of Ale-Hood (Old Icelandic)

Old Icelandic	Literal	English
# 4	# 4	# 4
Annan dag eftir gekk Broddi til búðar Þorkels Geitssonar og inn í búðina og kastaði orðum á Þorkel.	Next day after went Broddi to booth Thorkell Geitsson's and into booth and cast words to Thorkell.	The next day afterwards Broddi went to Thorkell Geitisson's booth and exchanged words with Thorkell.
Hann svaraði fá og var hinn reiðasti.	He answered few and was the most-angry.	He answered little and was very angry.
Broddi mælti:	Broddi spoke:	Broddi spoke:
"Því er eg hér kominn frændi að eg sá missmíð á því er eg talaði við þig.	"For am i here coming kinsman that i saw mistake in what was i said with you.	"For I have come here, kinsman, because I saw a mistake in what I said to you.
Vil eg þess biðja að þú virðir mér það til bernsku og ósvisku en látum eigi frændsemi okkar að verri.	Will i this ask that you value me that to childishness and unwise but let-us not kinship ours to worsen.	I wish to ask you, though you find me given to childishness, and unwise, let our kinship not worsen.
Er hér sverð búið er eg vil gefa þér.	Is here sword to-settle that i will give to-you.	Here is a sword that I will give to you to settle.
Vil eg að það fylgi að þú farir að heimboði til mín í sumar og skal það lýsa að eigi skulu betri gripir í minni eigu en þeir er þú skalt þiggja".	Will i to this follow that you travel to home-booth to mine in summer and shall that show that none shall better treasures of mine own than this that you shall receive".	I would like to follow this by inviting you to travel to my home booth in summer, and I will show you that I have no treasures finer than the ones that you shall receive here".
Þorkell tók þessu þakksamlega, sagði að hann var þess fús að þeir gerðu góða sína frændsemi.	Thorkell took these thankfully, said that he was this willing that they made good their kinship.	Thorkell took this gladly, and said that he was willing to make good their kinship.
Gekk þá Broddi heim.	Went then Broddi home.	Broddi then went home.
Það var aftaninn fyrir þinglausnir að Broddi gekk vestur yfir á en við brúarsporðinn hittast þeir Guðmundur og varð ekki að kveðjum.	That was back for assembly-ending that Broddi went west over river and with footbridge found they Gudmund and were not to greet.	It was the last day of the assembly that Broddi went west over the river, and at a footbridge he met Gudmund, and neither greeted the other.
Og er þeir skildust þá veik Guðmundur aftur og mælti:	And as they separated then gave Gudmund back and said:	And as they passed each other Gudmund looked back and said:

The Tale of Ale-Hood (Old Icelandic)

Old Icelandic	Literal	English
"Hverja leið skaltu ríða af þingi Broddi?" Hann sneri aftur og mælti:	"What way shall-you ride from assembly Broddi?" He turned back and said:	Which way will you ride back from the Assembly, Broddi?
"Ef þér er forvitni á því mun eg ríða um Kjöl til Skagafjarðar, þá til Eyjafjarðar, þaðan Ljósavatnsskarð og svo til Mývatns og síðan Möðrudalsheiði".	"If you are curious of then shall i ride about Kjol to Skagafjord, then to Eyjafjord, from-there Ljosavatnsskard and so to Mywater and after Morudale-moor".	He turned back and said: "If you are curious then I shall ride around Kjol to Skagafjord, then to Eyafjord, and from there to Ljosavatnsskard and so on to Mywater, and after that Morudale-Moor".
Guðmundur mælti:	Gudmund said:	Gudmind said:
"Efn orð þín og ríð Ljósavatnsskarð".	"Carry-out words yours and ride Ljosavatnsskard".	Carry out your words and ride through Ljosavatnsskard.
Broddi segir:	Broddi said:	Broddi said:
"Efna skal það eða ætlar þú Guðmundur að verja mér skarðið? Allmjög eru þér þá mislagðar hendur ef þú varðar mér Ljósavatnsskarð svo að eg megi þar eigi fara með förunautum mínum en þú varðar það eigi hið litla skarð sem er í milli þjóa þér svo að ámælislaust sé".	"Carry-out shall that but intend you Gudmund to guard me the-pass All-greatly are you then misplaced hand if you guard me Ljosavatnsskard such that i may there not travel with companions mine as you guarded that not the little gap as that in between buttocks yours so as without-reproach be".	"I shall carry that out, but do you intend to guard against me passing? You are greatly mistaken if you try to stop me at Ljosavatnsskard with my companions, as you failed to guard the little gap in your backside so as to be without reproach".
Skildust þeir við svo búið og spurðust þessi orð um allt þingið.	Separated they with so settled and asked these words about all assembly.	They separated and these words were learnt by all who were at the assembly.
En er Þorkell Geitsson varð þessa vís þá gekk hann til fundar við Brodda og bað að hann skyldi ríða Sandleið eða ella hið eystra".	When that Thorkell Geitisson was this aware then went he to meet with Brodda and bid that he should ride Sandy-road or otherwise the east".	When Thorkell Geitisson was aware of this, he went to meet with Broddi and invited that he "should ride on the sandy road or to the east".
Broddi segir:	Broddi said:	Broddi said:
"Eg mun ríða þá leið er eg hefi sagt Guðmundi því að hann mun virða mér til hugleysis ef eg fer eigi svo".	"I would ride then way that i have said Gudmund because that he should worth me to cowardice if i travel not so".	I should ride the way that I told Gudmund I would, because otherwise he shall value me as a coward if I do not.

The Tale of Ale-Hood (Old Icelandic)

Old Icelandic	Literal	English
Þorkell mælti: "Við munum þá ríða báðir saman frændi og flokkur okkar lítill".	Thorkell said: "With should then ride both together kinsman and band ours little".	Thorkell said: "We should both ride together then, kinsman, and our little band".
Broddi sagði að honum þótti sæmd í föruneyti hans og lést það fjarna vilja.	Broddi said that he thought honour to companions his and burden that remove would.	Broddi said that he thought it a great honour to ride with him and his companions, and it would remove a burden.
Síðan ríða þeir Þorkell og Broddi báðir saman með flokka sína norður Öxnadalsheiði.	Afterwards rode they Thorkell and Broddi both together with band his north Oxnadale-moor.	Afterwards Thorkell and Broddi together with his band rode north to Oxnadale-Moor.
Voru þeir í einni ferð og Einar Eyjólfsson mágur Þorkels.	Was they on one journey and Einar Eyjolfsson brother-in-law Thorkell.	It was on the journey that Thorkell's father-in-law Einar Eyjolfsson joined them.
Riðu þeir Broddi og Þorkell til Þverár með Einari og voru þar um nótt.	Rode they Broddi and Thorkell to Thverriver with Einar and were there about night.	Broddi and Thorkell rode to Thverriver with Einar and stayed there for the night.
Síðan reið Einar á leið með þeim með fjölmenni mikið og skildust eigi fyrr en við Skjálfandafljót.	After riding Einar the way with them with followers many and separated not before about with Skjalfandi-River.	Afterwards Einar and his many followers rode with them, and they did not separate until they reached Skjalfandi River.
Reið þá Einar heim en þeir Þorkell og Broddi léttu eigi sinni ferð fyrr en þeir komu austur í Vopnafjörð til búa sinna.	Rode then Einar home about them Thorkell and Broddi relieved not their journey before that they came east to Vopnafjord to homes theirs.	Einar then rode home and then Thorkell and Broddi did not rest their journey until they came east to Vapnfjord to their homes.
Það sumar fór Þorkell að heimboði til Brodda frænda síns og þá þar allgóðar gjafir.	That summer travelled Thorkell to home-booth to Broddi kinsman his and then there all-good gifts.	That summer Thorkell travelled to the home-booth of his kinsman Broddi and then accepted all good gifts.
Höfðu þeir þá hina bestu frændsemi með vináttu og hélst það meðan þeir lifðu.	Had they then the best kinship with friendship and held that long-as they lived.	They then had the best kinship as long as they lived.
Og lýkur þar sögu Ölkofra.	And ends here the-saga Ale-Hood.	And here ends the saga of Ale-Hood.

Word List *(Old Icelandic to English)*

Old Icelandic	English

A, a

að	as, at, of, that, the, to, to-you
aðra	other, others
aðrir	other, others
af	from, of, of
afglapi	simpleton
aftaninn	back
aftur	back
alda	wave
aldur	age
allan	all, all, every
allfús	all-happy, all-happy
allgóðar	all-good
allir	all, all
allmikið	all-much
allmjög	all-greatly, all-greatly, all-much, all-much
allra	all
allt	all, all, altogether
allur	all, all
allvesallega	miserable
alnar	measures
alþýðu	the-people
andsvör	answer, answers
annað	other, other
annan	next
annar	another
annarri	another
annars	others
argaskatt	cowardly
auðsætt	obvious
augu	eyes
aumlega	abjectly
aumlegast	miserable
austur	east, east

Á, á

á	about, at, by, in, is, of, on, river, the, to
ábyrgjast	guarantee
áðan	earlier
ámælislaust	without-reproach
ást	affection
átt	had, had, owned
átti	had
áttir	had
áttu	directions, had, have

Æ, æ

ær	awed
ætla	intend, suppose
ætlaði	intended
ætlar	intend

B, b

bað	asked, bid, invited
báðir	both
bæði	asked, both
baki	back
báru	bore
bauð	offered
beitast	employing
bernsku	childishness
best	best
besti	best
bestu	best
betri	better
beutr	better
bíða	wait
biðja	ask
biður	invited
birni	bear
Bjarnason	Bjarnason (name)
bjó	lived
Bláskógum	Blawoods (place)
Böðvarsdal	Bodvarsdale (place)
borði	borne
brá	drew

Word List (Old Icelandic to English)

Old Icelandic	English
brann	burned, burnt
brást	transformed
brátt	soon
brautargengi	path-assistance
brenna	burn
brenndi	burned
brenndir	burned
Brodda	Brodda (name), Brodda's (name), Broddi (name)
Brodd-Helgi	Brodd-Helgi (name)
Broddi	Broddi (name)
brott	away
brúarsporðinn	footbridge
brunnu	burned
brýn	urgent
búa	homes, settle
búða	booths
búðar	booth, booths
búðarvegginum	booth-walls
búðina	booth
búðinni	booth, booths
búið	settled, to-settle
búist	prepared
burst	cheated

D, d

Old Icelandic	English
dæma	deem
dæmdir	deem
dag	day
daga	days
daginn	the-day
deila	share, sharing
deildust	judged
drambi	arrogance
dregið	drawn
dregin	drawn
drengskapur	word-of-honour
drepa	kill
drepinn	killed
drifu	flocked
drjúgir	substantial
dró	drew
duga	help
dugið	enough
dugnað	assistance
dvaldist	dwelled
dylja	disguise
dýrlegu	dearly

E, e

Old Icelandic	English
eða	but, or
ef	if
efn	carry-out
efna	carry-out
eftir	after, behind, later
eftirförina	after-travelling
eg	i
eiga	have, said-of
eigi	no, none, not, not-of, only
eigngirni	selfish
eigu	own
ein	only
Einar	Einar (name)
Einari	Einar (name)
einmæli	one-talk
einn	one
einni	one
einu	one
einurð	determined
Eiríkssyni	Eriksson (name)
eitt	one
ekki	not
eldur	fire
eldurinn	fire
ella	otherwise
en	about, and, as, but, in, than, that, the, then, when
enda	in-the-end
engi	no, none
engu	none
er	am, are, as, be, i, is, that, the, then, was, were, when, which, who
erindi	errand

Word List (Old Icelandic to English)

Old Icelandic	English
ert	are
eru	are, they, was, were
Eyjafjarðar	Eyjafjord (place)
Eyjólfsson	Eyjolfsson (name), son-of-Eyjolf (name)
Eyjólfur	Eyjolf (name)
eystra	east

É, é

ég	i

F, f

Old Icelandic	English
fá	few
faðir	father
færi	opportunity
fæturna	feet
falli	fall
fallinn	fall
fangi	enemies
fara	travel
farir	travel
fastur	fastened
fé	fee, money
feginn	relieved
féið	fee
fekk	got
fékk	got
félaga	companions
félitlir	fee-little
féll	fell
felldur	fall
fengið	got
fer	go, travel
ferð	go, journey, travelled
festist	fastened
févænlegt	money-promising
fimmti	fifth
fingrum	fingers
firn	awful
fjandskap	fiend-ship
fjár	wealth
fjáreigandi	property-owning
fjárlægir	financial
fjarna	remove
fjölmenni	followers
fjórði	fourth
flokka	band
flokkur	band
föður	father
fól	fool
for	for
fór	travelled
forðað	avoided
fórst	travelled
fóru	travelled
fórum	travelled
förunauta	companions
förunautar	companions
förunautum	companions
föruneyti	companions
forvitni	curious
fóta	feet
frá	from
frænda	kinsman, kinsmen
frændi	kinsman, kinsmen
frændsemi	kinship
fram	from, from-forward
fullting	assistance
fundar	meet
fundið	found
fús	willing
fylgi	follow
fyrir	before, by, for, therefore
fyrr	before
fyrst	first

G, g

Old Icelandic	English
gæta	guarded
gæti	got
gáfu	gave
gagns	benefit
ganga	go, to-go, went
gefa	give
Geitisson	Geitisson (name), son-of-Geiti (name)

Word List (Old Icelandic to English)

Old Icelandic	English
Geitsson	Geitisson (name)
Geitssonar	Geitisson's (name)
gekk	went
gellis	gellir
gengið	walked
gengu	went
gera	be, be-done, do, made, make, to-do
gerð	made
gerðar	do
gerði	did, done, made
gerðina	make
gerðinni	make
gerðist	happened
gerðu	made
gerið	make
gerist	was
gert	done
gerum	be, being, doing, make
get	get
gettu	getting
gjafir	gifts
gjaldast	be-paid, pay
glámsýni	big-mistake
góð	good
góða	good
goðana	chieftans
goðar	chieftans
Goðaskógur	Godaskogur (place)
goði	chieftan
góðs	chieftans, good
góðu	good
göfulegri	nobler
goldið	paid
grátfeginn	weeping-for-joy
grét	wept
grimmu	grim
gripir	treasures
gröfunum	pit
Guðdala-Starri	Guddala-Starri (name)
Guðmund	Gudmund (name)
Guðmundar	Gudmund (name)
Guðmundi	Gudmund (name)
Guðmundur	Gudmund (name)

H, h

Old Icelandic	English
hætta	end
hættir	mannered
hafa	have
hafði	had
hafið	have
hafir	have
hagur	handy
halanum	tail-wagging
halda	hold
Hallsson	Hallsson (name)
handlagi	agreement
handlaginu	handshake
handsala	confirm
handsalsvætti	agreement
hann	he, him, it
hans	him, his
hátt	way
haust	autumn
haustið	autumn
hefðu	had
hefi	have
hefir	has, have
hefna	revenge
hefnir	avenge
hefur	has
heim	home
heimboði	home-booth
heita	call
heiti	named
heitinn	named
heldur	rather
helst	held
hélst	held
hendur	hand
hér	here
héraða	districts
héruð	district, districts
hesturinn	horse
hét	was-named
hið	the, then
hina	the, then
hinir	other

Word List (Old Icelandic to English)

Old Icelandic	English
hinn	the
hinum	others
hitt	find, found
hittast	found, meet
hitti	found
hjá	beside
hjálpa	help
hjálpið	help
hljóp	ran
hlut	lot
hluta	lot
hlýða	listen
hnæfilyrðum	blows
höfði	head
höfðingja	chieftans
höfðingjarnir	chieftans
höfðu	had, owned
höfum	have
honum	he, him, his, to-him
hræddur	scared
Hrafnabjörgum	Hrafnabjorg (place)
hrapa	hurry
hraunið	lava-fields
hraustur	brave
hug	mind
hugleysis	cowardice
hún	she
hvaðan	where
hvar	where
hvass	sharp
hver	who
hverja	what
hverjum	each, whether
hvern	each
hvers	each
hversu	how, how-so
hvert	which
hví	why
hvort	either, whether
hyggja	think

I, i

Old Icelandic	English
iðju	occupation
iðn	craft
illa	ill
illt	ill
illyrðum	malice
inn	in
inn´i	into
itl	little

Í, í

Old Icelandic	English
í	about, among, as, at, in, of, on, that, the, to, with
íþróttamaður	sports-man

J, j

Old Icelandic	English
jafnan	equally
jafnstórlega	equally-great
jarðar	earth
járn	iron

K, k

Old Icelandic	English
kæmu	came
kæra	accuse
kalla	call
kallað	called
kallaður	called
kann	can, known
kápuna	cloak
kastaði	cast
kastar	cast
kaup	bought, buy
kaupa	bought, buy
kemur	come
kenn	know
keypt	bought
keyptu	bought
Kjöl	Kjol (place)
kjörið	choice
kjörir	choice
kjósa	choose
klengisök	small-blame

Word List (Old Icelandic to English)

Old Icelandic	English
kofra	hood
kol	coal
kola	coal
kolbrennu	coal-burning
kölluðu	called
kom	came
koma	came, come, coming
komið	comes, coming
kominn	coming
komnir	coming
komu	came
komumst	come
konu	wife
kost	benefit
kostur	choice
kraup	kneeled
kunna	know
kvað	said
kveðjum	greet
kýs	choose

L, l

lætur	behaviour
lagði	laid
lagðist	laid
lagt	laid
láta	leave, let
látum	let, let-us
launanna	loans
leggja	allow
leggur	lay
leið	during, way
leiða	objection
leitað	sought
leitar	seek
lengi	long, longer
lést	burden, let
lét	let
lettara	easier
léttu	relieved
lið	assistance, company, help
líða	passed
liði	help

Old Icelandic	English
liðs	help, people
liðveilsunni	supportive
lifðu	lived
liggir	laying
líkar	alike
líkast	likely
limið	foliage
líst	beholding, like
lítill	little, small
lítilræði	little-advised
lítils	little
litla	little
lítt	little
Ljósavatnsskarð	Ljosavatnsskard (place)
ljótur	ugly
lofar	praises
lög	law
logaði	blazed
Lögbergi	Law-Rock (place)
Lögbergs	Law-Rock (place)
lögmaður	law-speaker
lögréttu	law-assembly
lögréttuna	law-assembly
lögskil	legal-settlement
lokið	ended
Lönguhlíð	Langahlid (place)
lúka	finish
lúkum	conclude
lykt	conclusion
lýkur	ends
lýsa	show
lýsir	declared

M, m

má	may
maður	a-man, man
mæla	matters
mælir	speaks, talking
mælti	said, spoke
mætli	said, spoke
mág	brother-in-law
mágur	brother-in-law
mál	matter, the-matter

Word List (Old Icelandic to English)

Old Icelandic	English
málaefni	matters
máli	matter, speak
málið	matter, the-matter
málinu	case
málkunnigur	talking-known
málóði	of-strong-language
máls	matter
mann	man, men
manna	men
mannamunur	integrity
manni	man
manns	man's
mannsektir	fines
mansöngsdrápu	love-song-poem
marga	many
margir	many
markaði	marked
mart	many
mátti	may
máttir	may
með	among, it, with
meðan	long-as
megi	may
meigu	may
meira	more
menn	man, many, men, people
mér	i, me, of-me, to, to-me
merarlíki	mare-like
merin	mare
mest	most
mig	me
mikið	many
mikil	great, much
miklir	great
milli	between
mín	mine
mína	mine
minn	mine
minni	mine
minnisamt	memorable
mínu	my
mínum	mine
misjafnt	uneven-in
mislagðar	misplaced
missmíð	mistake
missýni	mistake
missýnist	mistake
mitt	my
mjög	much
Möðrudalsheiði	Morudale-moor (place)
mögur	skinny
mönnum	men
mörgum	many
mun	shall, should, would
mundi	could, would
mundu	would
mungát	ale
mungátin	ale
muni	should, would
munir	should
muntu	should
munu	should, will
munuð	shall
munum	should
mútugjafir	bribes
Mývatns	Mywater (place)

N, n

Old Icelandic	English
næði	neared
næst	nearest, next
næsta	next-to
næstir	nearest
nafn	name
nafndrægur	named
nafni	the-name
nefi	nose, noses
nefndi	named
nefndir	name
nefndur	named
neitaði	refusal, refused
nema	take, taking
niðurfall	dropping
nokkuð	some, something
nokkura	some
nokkurar	some
nokkurir	some
nokkurn	someone
nokkuru	somewhat

Word List (Old Icelandic to English)

Old Icelandic	English
norðu	north
norður	north
nótt	night
nóttina	night
nú	not, now
nytja	use

O, o

ofan	over
ofarlega	high-up
oft	often
oftlega	often
ofureflismenn	ultra-strong-men
og	also, and
okkar	ours
okkart	ours
okkra	ours
okkur	ours, us
orð	word, words
orða	words
orðið	word
orðinn	become
orðum	words
ormur	orm
ortir	worded
oss	ours, us, we

Ó, ó

ógæfu	un-giving
óhæfan	trouble
ólíklegt	unlike
ómaklegur	uncomfortable
ópið	open
óvinum	un-friends
ovisku	unwise

Ö, ö

öðrum	other, others
öl	ale
Ölkofra	Ale-Hood (name), Ale-hood's (name)
Ölkofri	Ale-Hood (name)
öll	all
öllu	all
önnur	another
örhjarta	un-heartened
Öxnadalsheiði	Oxnadale-moor (place)
öxnina	oxen
öxnum	oxen

R, r

ráð	advice, counsel, matter
ráði	counsel
ráðið	decided
ráðinn	decided
ræddi	discussed
ræddu	discussed
rakkara	bolder
ráku	drove
rán	robbery
rann	runs
Rauða-Bjarnarson	son-of-Rauda-Bjarn (name)
regin	ruling
reið	riding, rode
reiðasti	most-angry
reiðst	counsel, riding, rode
reikuðu	roamed
réttlátir	right-like
reytti	tried
ríð	ride
ríða	ride, rode
riðu	rode

S, s

sá	saw, so, that
sæli	good
sæll	happy
sæmd	honour
sæmdunum	honour

Word List (Old Icelandic to English)

Old Icelandic	English	Old Icelandic	English
sætt	settlement	*sjálfdæmi*	self-judgement
saga	story	*sjálfur*	himself
sagði	said	*skaða*	damages
sagt	said, told	*Skafta*	Skafti (name)
sakferlum	lawsuits	*Skafti*	Skafti (name)
sama	same	*Skagafjarðar*	Skagafjord (place)
saman	together	*skal*	shall
sandleið	sandy-road	*skalt*	shall
sanns	the-truth	*skaltu*	shall-you
sástu	saw-you	*skarð*	gap
sat	sat	*skarðið*	the-pass
satt	TRUE	*skáru*	cut
sátt	settlement	*skildust*	separated
sátu	sat	*skilið*	divided, understood
sáu	this	*skilt*	divided
sé	as, be, being, see, so	*skipta*	exchange
segir	said	*Skjálfandafljót*	Skjalfandi-River (place)
segja	said, say	*sköðum*	damage
seint	late	*skóg*	forest
sekja	seek	*skóga*	forest
sektar	guilt	*skógabrennuna*	forest-burning
seldu	sold	*skógana*	forests
selfeitan	fat	*skógar*	forests
selja	sell	*skógarmanns*	outlawry
sem	as, me, so, that, which	*skóggang*	outlawry
sendi	sent	*skóginn*	forest
sendiboð	messenger	*skógur*	forest
sér	him, himself, his, theirs, themselves	*skríða*	action
		skulu	shall
sétti	sixth	*skuluð*	should
sex	six	*skulum*	should
síðan	after, afterwards, since, then	*skyldi*	should, wished
		skyldu	should
Síðu-Hallssonar	son-of-Sidu-Hall (name)	*skyldum*	should
		skýrst	clarified
siður	custom	*skýrt*	clear
sín	theirs, they	*slauðraði*	trailing-behind
sína	his, their	*slík*	such
sínkur	stingy	*slíka*	such
sinn	his	*slíkt*	so, such
sinna	theirs	*slíkum*	such
sinni	his, opinion, their	*slitu*	dissolved
síns	his	*sneri*	turned
sitja	sit	*snökta*	sob
sjá	saw, so, this	*Snorri*	Snorri (name)

Word List (Old Icelandic to English)

Old Icelandic	English
snýrð	turned
sofnaði	slept
sögðu	said
sögðust	said
sogört	saying
sögu	the-saga
sögunni	the-saga
sökina	seeking
sökum	blame
sökunautur	defendant
son	son
spurði	asked
spurðust	asked
spurt	asked
ssem	as
staðfest	confirmed
stalst	stealing
Starri	Starri (name)
stefndi	summons, summonsed
stefnu	summons
stefnudagar	policy-days
stefnuför	summons
Steingrímur	Steingrim (name)
stikað	stitched
stóð	stood
stóðhest	stallion
stórlæti	pride
stórleika	pride
stórmenni	great-men
stórorðu	high-sounding
stúf	stump
stundir	awhile
stundu	awhile
stungist	wounded
sú	yours
sumar	summer
sumarið	summer
sundur	asunder
svaraði	answered
svarar	answered
sverð	sword
Sviðningi	Svidning (place)
svo	so, such
svöruðu	answered
svörum	answers

Old Icelandic	English
sýnast	appear
synjað	refused

T, t

Old Icelandic	English
tæki	took
taka	take
takast	took
talaði	said
telja	tell
tíðinda	news
tíðindi	news
til	about, for, to
tiltækilegra	available
tíma	time
tók	took
tré	wood
trefill	trefill
tvítugsaldri	twenty-aged
tvo	two

Þ, þ

Old Icelandic	English
þá	then
það	it, that, the, this, to, with
þaðan	from-there
þakksamlega	thankfully
þann	that, then
þar	here, there
þau	his, they
þegar	as-soon-as, straightaway, straight-away, then
þeim	them, these, they, those
þeir	them, they, this
þeirra	of-the, their, theirs, them, they, those
þenna	that, this
þér	then, to-you, you, yours
þess	this
þessa	this
þessar	this

Word List (Old Icelandic to English)

Old Icelandic	English
þessi	these, this
þessu	these, this
þetta	it, that, this
þið	you
þig	you
þiggja	receive
þín	yours
þingi	assembly
þingið	assembly
þinglausnir	assembly-ending
þingmenn	assembly, assembly-men
þings	assembly
þingum	assembly
þinn	you, yours
þinni	yours
þíns	yours
þitt	yours
þjóa	buttocks
þó	though
þoli	tolerate
Þórðar	Thord (name)
Þórðarson	Thordarson (name)
Þórhalldur	Thorhall (name)
Þórhallsstöðum	Thorhallsstead (place)
Þórhallur	Thorhall (name)
þori	greater-part
Þorkel	Thorkell (name)
Þorstein	Thorstein (name)
Þorsteinn	Thorstein (name)
Þorsteins	Thorstein (name), Thorstein's (name)
þót	though
þótt	though, thought
þótti	seem, seemed, thought
þóttist	thought
þriðji	third
þú	you, your
þung	heavy
þungs	heavily
þurfa	need
þverafæti	foot-around
Þverár	Thverriver (place)
því	as, because, for, of, since, then, therefore, what, with
þykir	seems, think
þykjast	consider

U, u

Old Icelandic	English
um	about, around, in, of, over
undir	from-beneath, under
upp	up

Ú, ú

Old Icelandic	English
úr	from, of, out-of
út	from, out, out-of

V, v

Old Icelandic	English
vaðmál	homespun-cloth
vænta	expect
væri	would-be
væru	were
vaknaði	awoke
vakti	woke
vandast	difficult
vanir	friends
var	then, was, were
varaðist	warned
varð	became, was, were
varða	concerning
varðar	guard, guarded
varðstu	were-you
varið	defend
varst	were
Vatnsdal	Vatnsdal (place)
veg	way
veginn	killed
vegur	way
veifiskati	spendthrift
veik	gave
veit	know

Word List (Old Icelandic to English)

Old Icelandic	English	*Old Icelandic*	English
veita	grant, know, provide	vorþings	local-assembly
veitið	know	voru	are, was, were
veitti	granted	voruð	were
veittu	grant	votta	witness
vel	well	vottar	witnesses
vér	we	vottnefna	witnesses
vera	be		
verð	deserve		
verða	being, was, were		
verður	worth		

Y, y

Old Icelandic	English
verið	been
verja	guard
verr	worse
verri	worsen
vert	worth
vestur	west
veturinn	winter
við	on, we, with
víða	many, widely
viðinn	trees
vil	will
vildi	willed, wills
vilja	willed, wish, would
vilji	willing
viljið	will
viljum	will
vill	will, wishes
vilnað	willed
vináttu	friendship
vindur	wind
vini	friends
vinir	friends
vinsæl	popularity
virða	worth
virðir	value
vís	aware
vita	knowing
vitrir	wise
voðaverk	accidents
völluna	plains
von	hope, wished
Vopnafjörð	Vopnafjord (place)
vor	our, spring
vorkunn	pity
vorra	talking-loudly

Old Icelandic	English
yðra	yours
yðrum	yours
yður	yours
yðvarn	your
yfir	across, over
ykkur	you
yppa	up
yrðu	be

Word List *(English to Old Icelandic)*

English	Old Icelandic
A, a	
about	á, á, á, á, á
at	á, á, á
as	að, að, áðan, ær, ætla, ætlaði, ætlar, af
awed	ær
age	aldur
all	allan, allan, allan, allfús, allfús, allgóðar, allir, allir, allmikið, allmjög, allmjög
all-happy	allfús, allfús
all-good	allgóðar
all-much	allmikið, allmjög, allmjög
all-greatly	allmjög, allmjög
altogether	allt
answer	andsvör
answers	andsvör, annar
another	annar, annarri, argaskatt
affection	ást
abjectly	aumlega
asked	bað, bað, bað, báðir, bæði
ask	biðja
away	brott
arrogance	drambi
assistance	dugnað, dvaldist, dylja
after	eftir, eftir
after-travelling	eftirförina
and	en, en
am	er
are	er, er, er, er
awful	firn
avoided	forðað
agreement	handlagi, handlaginu
autumn	haust, haustið
avenge	hefnir
among	í, í
accuse	kæra
allow	leggja
alike	líkar
a-man	maður
ale	mungát, mungátin, mútugjafir
also	og
Ale-Hood (name)	Ölkofra, Ölkofra
Ale-hood's (name)	Ölkofra
advice	ráð
afterwards	síðan
action	skríða
awhile	stundir, stundu
asunder	sundur
answered	svaraði, svarar, svöruðu
appear	sýnast
as-soon-as	þegar
assembly	þingi, þingið, þinglausnir, þingmenn, þingmenn
assembly-ending	þinglausnir
assembly-men	þingmenn
available	tiltækilegra
around	um
awoke	vaknaði
aware	vís
accidents	voðaverk
across	yfir
B, b	
by	á, á
back	aftaninn, aftur, aldur
bid	bað
both	báðir, bæði
bore	báru
best	best, besti, bestu
better	betri, beutr
bear	birni
Bjarnason (name)	Bjarnason
Blawoods (place)	Bláskógum
Bodvarsdale (place)	Böðvarsdal
borne	borði

Word List (English to Old Icelandic)

English	*Old Icelandic*	English	*Old Icelandic*
burned	brann, brann, brenna, brenndi	# C, c	
burnt	brann	cowardly	argaskatt
burn	brenna	childishness	bernsku
Brodda (name)	Brodda	cheated	burst
Brodda's (name)	Brodda	carry-out	efn, efna
Broddi (name)	Brodda, Brodd-Helgi	companions	félaga, félitlir, féll, felldur, fengið
Brodd-Helgi (name)	Brodd-Helgi	curious	forvitni
booths	búða, búðar, búðar	chieftans	goðana, goðar, Goðaskógur, goði, góðs
booth	búðar, búðar, búðarvegginum		
booth-walls	búðarvegginum	chieftan	goði
but	eða, ef	confirm	handsala
behind	eftir	call	heita, helst
be	er, er, er, erindi, ert, eru	cowardice	hugleysis
band	flokka, flokkur	craft	iðn
before	fyrir, fyrir	came	kæmu, kæra, kalla, kallað
benefit	gagns, ganga		
be-done	gera	called	kallað, kallaður, kann
being	gerum, gerum, gerum	can	kann
be-paid	gjaldast	cloak	kápuna
big-mistake	glámsýni	cast	kastaði, kastar
beside	hjá	come	kemur, kenn, keypt
blows	hnæfilyrðum	choice	kjörið, kjörir, kjósa
brave	hraustur	choose	kjósa, kofra
bought	kaup, kaup, kaupa, kaupa	coal	kol, kola
		coal-burning	kolbrennu
buy	kaup, kaupa	coming	koma, komið, komið, kominn
behaviour	lætur		
burden	lést	comes	komið
beholding	líst	company	lið
blazed	logaði	conclude	lúkum
brother-in-law	mág, mágur	conclusion	lykt
between	milli	case	málinu
bribes	mútugjafir	could	mundi
become	orðinn	counsel	ráð, ráð, ráði
bolder	rakkara	custom	siður
blame	sökum	cut	skáru
buttocks	þjóa	clarified	skýrst
because	því	clear	skýrt
became	varð	confirmed	staðfest
been	verið	consider	þykjast
		concerning	varða

Word List (English to Old Icelandic)

English	Old Icelandic

D, d

English	Old Icelandic
directions	áttu
drew	brá, brann
deem	dæma, dæmdir
day	dag
days	daga
drawn	dregið, dregin
dwelled	dvaldist
disguise	dylja
dearly	dýrlegu
determined	einurð
do	gera, gera
did	gerði
done	gerði, gerði
doing	gerum
districts	héraða, héruð
district	héruð
during	leið
declared	lýsir
dropping	niðurfall
decided	ráðið, ráðinn
discussed	ræddi, ræddu
drove	ráku
damages	skaða
divided	skilið, skilt
damage	sköðum
dissolved	slitu
defendant	sökunautur
difficult	vandast
defend	varið
deserve	verð

E, e

English	Old Icelandic
earlier	áðan
every	allan
eyes	augu
east	austur, austur, bað
employing	beitast
enough	dugið
Einar (name)	Einar, Einari
Eriksson (name)	Eiríkssyni
errand	erindi
Eyjafjord (place)	Eyjafjarðar
Eyjolfsson (name)	Eyjólfsson
Eyjolf (name)	Eyjólfur
enemies	fangi
end	hætta
each	hverjum, hvern, hvers
either	hvort
equally	jafnan
equally-great	jafnstórlega
earth	jarðar
easier	lettara
ended	lokið
ends	lýkur
exchange	skipta
expect	vænta

F, f

English	Old Icelandic
from	af, aftaninn, aftur, aldur, allan
footbridge	brúarsporðinn
flocked	drifu
fire	eldur, eldurinn
few	fá
father	faðir, fæturna
feet	fæturna, falli
fall	falli, fallinn, fangi
fastened	fastur, fé
fee	fé, fé
fee-little	félitlir
fell	féll
fifth	fimmti
fingers	fingrum
fiend-ship	fjandskap
financial	fjárlægir
followers	fjölmenni
fourth	fjórði
fool	fól
for	for, forðað, förunauta, förunautar
from-forward	fram
found	fundið, fylgi, fyrir, fyrir
follow	fylgi
first	fyrst
find	hitt

80

Word List (English to Old Icelandic)

English	*Old Icelandic*
foliage	*limið*
finish	*lúka*
fines	*mannsektir*
fat	*selfeitan*
forest	*skóg, skóga, skógabrennuna, skógana*
forest-burning	*skógabrennuna*
forests	*skógana, skógar*
from-there	*þaðan*
foot-around	*þverafæti*
from-beneath	*undir*
friends	*vanir, varð, varða*
friendship	*vináttu*

G, g

English	*Old Icelandic*
guarantee	*ábyrgjast*
got	*fekk, fékk, félaga, félitlir*
go	*fer, ferð, ferð*
guarded	*gæta, gæti*
gave	*gáfu, gagns*
give	*gefa*
Geitisson (name)	*Geitisson, Geitsson*
Geitisson's (name)	*Geitssonar*
gellir	*gellis*
get	*get*
getting	*gettu*
gifts	*gjafir*
good	*góð, góða, goðana, goðar, Goðaskógur*
Godaskogur (place)	*Goðaskógur*
grim	*grimmu*
Guddala-Starri (name)	*Guðdala-Starri*
Gudmund (name)	*Guðmund, Guðmundar, Guðmundi, Guðmundur*
greet	*kveðjum*
great	*mikil, mikil*
guilt	*sektar*
gap	*skarð*
great-men	*stórmenni*
greater-part	*þori*

English	*Old Icelandic*
guard	*varðar, varðar*
grant	*veita, veita*
granted	*veitti*

H, h

English	*Old Icelandic*
had	*átt, átt, átti, áttir, áttu, áttu, áttu, augu*
have	*áttu, augu, aumlega, aumlegast, austur, austur, bað, bað*
homes	*búa*
help	*duga, dugið, dugnað, dvaldist, dylja, dýrlegu*
happened	*gerðist*
handy	*hagur*
hold	*halda*
Hallsson (name)	*Hallsson*
handshake	*handlaginu*
he	*hann, hann*
him	*hann, hann, hans, hans*
his	*hans, haust, haustið, hefðu, hefi, hefir, hefir, hefnir*
has	*hefir, hefir*
home	*heim*
home-booth	*heimboði*
held	*helst, hélst*
hand	*hendur*
here	*hér, héraða*
horse	*hesturinn*
head	*höfði*
Hrafnabjorg (place)	*Hrafnabjörgum*
hurry	*hrapa*
how	*hversu*
how-so	*hversu*
hood	*kofra*
high-up	*ofarlega*
happy	*sæll*
honour	*sæmd, sæmdunum*
himself	*sér, sér*
high-sounding	*stórorðu*
heavy	*þung*
heavily	*þungs*
homespun-cloth	*vaðmál*

Word List (English to Old Icelandic)

English	*Old Icelandic*	English	*Old Icelandic*
hope	*von*	listen	*hlýða*
		lava-fields	*hraunið*
I, i		little	*itl, jafnan, jafnstórlega, jarðar, járn*
in	*á, á, ábyrgjast, að, að*	laid	*lagði, lagðist, lagt*
is	*á, ábyrgjast*	leave	*láta*
intend	*ætla, ætlaði*	let	*láta, látum, látum, launanna*
intended	*ætlaði*		
invited	*bað, báðir*	let-us	*látum*
if	*ef*	loans	*launanna*
i	*eg, ég, eiga, Einar*	lay	*leggur*
in-the-end	*enda*	long	*lengi*
it	*hann, hans, hans, haust*	longer	*lengi*
		laying	*liggir*
ill	*illa, illt*	likely	*líkast*
into	*inn´i*	like	*líst*
iron	*járn*	little-advised	*lítilræði*
integrity	*mannamunur*	Ljosavatnsskard (place)	*Ljósavatnsskarð*
J, j		law	*lög*
		Law-Rock (place)	*Lögbergi, Lögbergs*
judged	*deildust*	law-speaker	*lögmaður*
journey	*ferð*	law-assembly	*lögréttu, lögréttuna*
		legal-settlement	*lögskil*
K, k		Langahlid (place)	*Lönguhlíð*
		love-song-poem	*mansöngsdrápu*
kill	*drepa*	long-as	*meðan*
killed	*drepinn, drifu*	lawsuits	*sakferlum*
kinsman	*frænda, frænda*	late	*seint*
kinsmen	*frænda, frændi*	local-assembly	*vorþings*
kinship	*frændsemi*		
known	*kann*	**M, m**	
know	*kenn, keypt, keyptu, Kjöl, kjörið*	miserable	*allvesallega, alnar*
		measures	*alnar*
Kjol (place)	*Kjöl*	money	*fé*
kneeled	*kraup*	money-promising	*févænlegt*
knowing	*vita*	meet	*fundar, fundið*
		made	*gera, gera, gerð, gerðar*
L, l			
		make	*gera, gerð, gerðar, gerði, gerði*
lived	*bjó, Bláskógum*		
later	*eftir*	mannered	*hættir*
lot	*hlut, hluta*	mind	*hug*
		malice	*illyrðum*

Word List (English to Old Icelandic)

English	Old Icelandic
may	má, maður, maður, mæla, mág
man	maður, mæla, mág, mágur
matters	mæla, mág
matter	mál, málaefni, máli, málið, málinu
men	mann, manna, mannamunur, manni
man's	manns
many	marga, margir, markaði, mart, mátti, máttir, með
marked	markaði
more	meira
me	mér, merarlíki, merin
mare-like	merarlíki
mare	merin
most	mest
much	mikil, miklir
mine	mín, mína, minn, minni, minnisamt
memorable	minnisamt
my	mínu, mínum
misplaced	mislagðar
mistake	missmíð, missýni, missýnist
Morudale-moor (place)	Möðrudalsheiði
Mywater (place)	Mývatns
most-angry	reiðasti
messenger	sendiboð

N, n

English	Old Icelandic
next	annan, annars
no	eigi, eigi
none	eigi, eigi, eigi
not	eigi, eigi, eigi
not-of	eigi
nobler	göfulegri
named	heiti, heitinn, heldur, hét, hið
neared	næði
nearest	næst, næst
next-to	næsta
name	nafn, nafndrægur
nose	nefi
noses	nefi
north	norðu, norður
night	nótt, nóttina
now	nú
need	þurfa
news	tíðinda, tíðindi

O, o

English	Old Icelandic
of	á, á, á, á, á, að, að, að
on	á, á, á
other	aðra, aðra, aðrir, aðrir, ætla, af
others	aðra, aðrir, aðrir, ætla, af
owned	átt, auðsætt
obvious	auðsætt
offered	bauð
or	eða
only	eigi, eigngirni
own	eigu
one-talk	einmæli
one	einn, einni, einu, eitt
otherwise	ella
opportunity	færi
occupation	iðju
objection	leiða
of-strong-language	málóði
of-me	mér
over	ofan, oft, oftlega
often	oft, oftlega
ours	okkar, okkart, okkra, okkur, okkur
open	ópið
orm	ormur
Oxnadale-moor (place)	Öxnadalsheiði
oxen	öxnina, öxnum
opinion	sinni
outlawry	skógarmanns, skóggang
of-the	þeirra
out-of	úr, út
out	út

Word List (English to Old Icelandic)

English	Old Icelandic	English	Old Icelandic
our	*vor*		

P, p

English	Old Icelandic
path-assistance	*brautargengi*
prepared	*búist*
property-owning	*fjáreigandi*
pay	*gjaldast*
paid	*goldið*
pit	*gröfunum*
passed	*líða*
people	*liðs, liðveilsunni*
praises	*lofar*
policy-days	*stefnudagar*
pride	*stórlæti, stórleika*
provide	*veita*
popularity	*vinsæl*
plains	*völluna*
pity	*vorkunn*

R, r

English	Old Icelandic
river	*á*
relieved	*feginn, fer*
remove	*fjarna*
revenge	*hefna*
rather	*heldur*
ran	*hljóp*
refusal	*neitaði*
refused	*neitaði, nema*
robbery	*rán*
runs	*rann*
ruling	*regin*
riding	*reið, reið*
rode	*reið, reiðst, reiðst, reikuðu*
roamed	*reikuðu*
right-like	*réttlátir*
ride	*ríð, ríða*
receive	*þiggja*

S, s

English	Old Icelandic
suppose	*ætla*
simpleton	*afglapi*
soon	*brátt*
settle	*búa*
settled	*búið*
share	*deila*
sharing	*deila*
substantial	*drjúgir*
said-of	*eiga*
selfish	*eigngirni*
son-of-Eyjolf (name)	*Eyjólfsson*
son-of-Geiti (name)	*Geitisson*
scared	*hræddur*
she	*hún*
sharp	*hvass*
sports-man	*íþróttamaður*
small-blame	*klengisök*
said	*kvað, leið, leiða, leitað, leitar, léttu, líða, liðs, liðveilsunni, lítill*
sought	*leitað*
seek	*leitar, léttu*
supportive	*liðveilsunni*
small	*lítill*
show	*lýsa*
speaks	*mælir*
spoke	*mælti, mætli*
speak	*máli*
skinny	*mögur*
shall	*mun, mun, mun, mundi, mundu*
should	*mun, mun, mundi, mundu, muni, muni, munir, muntu, munu, munu, munuð*
some	*nokkuð, nokkuð, nokkura, nokkurar*
something	*nokkuð*
someone	*nokkurn*
somewhat	*nokkuru*
son-of-Rauda-Bjarn (name)	*Rauða-Bjarnarson*
saw	*sá, sá*

Word List (English to Old Icelandic)

English	Old Icelandic
so	sá, sá, sætt, saga, sagði, sagt
settlement	sætt, saga
story	saga
same	sama
sandy-road	sandleið
saw-you	sástu
sat	sat, satt
see	sé
say	segja
sold	seldu
sell	selja
sent	sendi
sixth	sétti
six	sex
since	síðan, síðan
son-of-Sidu-Hall (name)	Síðu-Hallssonar
stingy	sínkur
sit	sitja
self-judgement	sjálfdæmi
Skafti (name)	Skafta, Skafti
Skagafjord (place)	Skagafjarðar
shall-you	skaltu
separated	skildust
Skjalfandi-River (place)	Skjálfandafljót
such	slík, slíka, slíkt, slíkt, slíkum
sob	snökta
Snorri (name)	Snorri
slept	sofnaði
saying	sogört
seeking	sökina
son	son
stealing	stalst
Starri (name)	Starri
summons	stefndi, stefndi, stefnu
summonsed	stefndi
Steingrim (name)	Steingrímur
stitched	stikað
stood	stóð
stallion	stóðhest
stump	stúf
summer	sumar, sumarið
sword	sverð
Svidning (place)	Sviðningi
straightaway	þegar
straight-away	þegar
seem	þótti
seemed	þótti
seems	þykir
spendthrift	veifiskati
spring	vor

T, t

English	Old Icelandic
the	á, á, að, að, að, að, að, aðra, aðra
to	á, að, að, að, að, að
that	að, að, að, að, aðra, aðra, aðrir, aðrir, ætla, af
to-you	að, aðra
the-people	alþýðu
transformed	brást
to-settle	búið
the-day	daginn
than	en
then	en, en, engi, engi, engu, er, er, er, er, er, er
they	eru, eru, eru, Eyjólfsson, færi, fara
travel	fara, farir, feginn
travelled	ferð, fjár, fjáreigandi, fjarna, fór
therefore	fyrir, ganga
to-go	ganga
to-do	gera
treasures	gripir
tail-wagging	halanum
to-him	honum
think	hyggja, í
talking	mælir
the-matter	mál, máli
talking-known	málkunnigur
to-me	mér
the-name	nafni
take	nema, nema
taking	nema
trouble	óhæfan

Word List (English to Old Icelandic)

English	Old Icelandic
tried	reytti
told	sagt
together	saman
the-truth	sanns
true	
this	sáu, sé, sé, segir, segja, segja, sekja, seldu, selja, sem, sem
theirs	sér, sér, sétti, sex
themselves	sér
their	sína, sínkur, sinna
the-pass	skarðið
trailing-behind	slauðraði
turned	sneri, snökta
the-saga	sögu, sögunni
took	tæki, taka, takast
tell	telja
thankfully	þakksamlega
there	þar
them	þeim, þeim, þeim
these	þeim, þeim, þeim
those	þeim, þeir
though	þó, þoli, Þórðar
tolerate	þoli
Thord (name)	Þórðar
Thordarson (name)	Þórðarson
Thorhall (name)	Þórhalldur, Þórhallsstöðum
Thorhallsstead (place)	Þórhallsstöðum
Thorkell (name)	Þorkel
Thorstein (name)	Þorstein, Þorsteinn, Þorsteins
Thorstein's (name)	Þorsteins
thought	þótt, þótti, þótti
third	þriðji
Thverriver (place)	Þverár
time	tíma
trefill	trefill
twenty-aged	tvítugsaldri
two	tvo
trees	viðinn
talking-loudly	vorra

U, u

English	Old Icelandic
urgent	brýn
ugly	ljótur
uneven-in	misjafnt
use	nytja
ultra-strong-men	ofureflismenn
un-giving	ógæfu
us	okkur, ólíklegt
unlike	ólíklegt
uncomfortable	ómaklegur
un-heartened	örhjarta
un-friends	óvinum
unwise	ósvisku
understood	skilið
under	undir
up	upp, úr

V, v

English	Old Icelandic
Vatnsdal (place)	Vatnsdal
value	virðir
Vopnafjord (place)	Vopnafjörð

W, w

English	Old Icelandic
wave	alda
without-reproach	ámælislaust
wait	bíða
word-of-honour	drengskapur
when	en, engi
was	er, er, er, er, er, eru, eru
were	er, er, er, er, eru, eru, eru, Eyjólfsson, færi
which	er, er, eru
who	er, eru
wealth	fjár
willing	fús, fyrir
went	ganga, Geitisson, gekk
walked	gengið
weeping-for-joy	grátfeginn
wept	grét

Word List (English to Old Icelandic)

English	Old Icelandic	English	Old Icelandic
way	hátt, hefna, heiti, heitinn		
was-named	hét	**Y, y**	
where	hvaðan, hvar	yours	sú, sumar, sumarið, sverð, Sviðningi, svo, svo, synjað, tæki, taka
what	hverja, hverjum		
whether	hverjum, hvert		
why	hví		
with	í, iðju, íþróttamaður, klengisök, konu	you	þér, þér, þess, þessa, þessar, þessi
wife	konu	your	þú, þurfa
would	mun, mundi, mundu, muni, muni		
will	munu, munuð, munum, næði, næst		
word	orð, orð		
words	orð, orða, orðið		
worded	ortir		
we	oss, óvinum, ósvisku		
wished	skyldi, skyldu		
wounded	stungist		
wood	tré		
would-be	væri		
woke	vakti		
warned	varaðist		
were-you	varðstu		
well	vel		
worth	verður, verr, verri		
worse	verr		
worsen	verri		
west	vestur		
winter	veturinn		
widely	víða		
willed	vildi, vildi, vilja		
wills	vildi		
wish	vilja		
wishes	vill		
wind	vindur		
wise	vitrir		
witness	votta		
witnesses	vottar, vottnefna		

A Word Comparison of Old Norse and Old Icelandic Words

Old Norse	Old Icelandic	English
aftr	aftur	back
aldr	aldur	age
alla	allan	all
allfúss	allfús	all-happy
allmikit	allmikið	all-much
allmjök	allmjög	all-greatly
Allmjök	allmjög	all-much
allr	allur	all
Allvesalliga	allvesallega	miserable
álnir	alnar	measures
ámælilaust	ámælislaust	without-reproach
annarr	annar	another
annat	annað	other
annsvör	andsvör	answer
annsvör	andsvör	answers
at	að	as
at	að	at
at	að	of
at	að	that
at	að	the
at	að	to
at	að	to-you
átzt	ást	affection
aumliga	aumlega	abjectly
aumligast	aumlegast	miserable
austr	austur	east
berusku	bernsku	childishness
betr	beutr	better
bezt	best	best
bezta	bestu	best
bezti	besti	best
biðr	biður	invited
brátt	brást	transformed
brendi	brenndi	burned
Broddi	brá	drew
búða	búðar	booths
búðarveggnum	búðarvegginum	booth-walls
búit	búið	settled
búit	búið	to-settle
búizt	búist	prepared
bust	burst	cheated
dœma	dæma	deem
dœmdir	dæmdir	deem
dregit	dregið	drawn
drengskapr	drengskapur	word-of-honour
dugit	dugið	enough
dýrligu	dýrlegu	dearly
eðr	eða	but
eðr	eða	or
Eigi	eða	but
eigingirni	eigngirni	selfish
eigu	eiga	have
Einarr	einar	Einar (name)
Eirekssyni	eiríkssyni	Eriksson (name)
ek	eg	I
ek	ég	I
ek	og	and
ekkí	ekki	not
eldr	eldur	fire
Eldrinn	eldurinn	fire
Enn	en	about
Enn	en	and
Enn	en	as
enn	en	but
Enn	en	in
enn	en	than
Enn	en	that
enn	en	the
enn	en	then
Enn	en	when
er	að	that
Eyjólfr	eyjólfur	Eyjolf (name)
fastr	fastur	fastened
féit	féið	fee

A Word Comparison of Old Norse and Old Icelandic

Old Norse	Old Icelandic	English
fekk	fékk	got
feldr	felldur	fall
fell	féll	fell
fengit	fengið	got
ferr	ferð	go
févænligt	févænlegt	money-promising
fimti	fimmti	fifth
fjarlægir	fjárlægir	financial
flokkr	flokkur	band
føri	færi	opportunity
fœtrna	fæturna	feet
Fór	for	for
forðat	forðað	avoided
fórt	fórst	travelled
föruneyti	förunauta	companions
frammi	fram	from-forward
fundit	fundið	found
fúss	fús	willing
fyrir	frá	from
Geitisson	geitsson	Geitisson (name)
Geitissonar	geitssonar	Geitisson's (name)
gekk	fekk	got
gengit	gengið	walked
gerði	gerðu	made
gerðist	gerist	was
gerim	gerum	be
gerim	gerum	being
gerim	gerum	doing
gerim	gerum	make
gerit	gerið	make
gettú	gettu	getting
gjarna	fjarna	remove
goðar	þeir	they
Goðaskógr	goðaskógur	Godaskogur (place)
Goðdala-Starri	guðdala-starri	Guddala-Starri (name)
göfigligri	göfulegri	nobler
goldit	goldið	paid
Guðmundr	guðmundur	Gudmund (name)
Hafði	hann	he
hafim	höfum	have
hafit	hafið	have
hagr	hagur	handy
handlaginu	handlagi	agreement
handsalsvætti	handsalsvætti	agreement
haustit	haustið	autumn
hefði	hafði	had
hefði	hefðu	had
hefir	hefur	has
heldr	heldur	rather
helzt	helst	held
helzt	hélst	held
hendr	hendur	hand
hér	hann	he
heraða	héraða	districts
heruð	héruð	district
heruð	héruð	districts
hestrinn	hesturinn	horse
hit	hið	the
hit	hið	then
hittust	hittast	found
hjálpit	hjálpið	help
hnœfilyrðum	hnæfilyrðum	blows
hœttir	hættir	mannered
hræddr	hræddur	scared
hraunit	hraunið	lava-fields
hraustr	hraustur	brave
Hvárt	hvert	which
hvárt	hvort	either
hvárt	hvort	whether
Hverr	hver	who
hveru	hvern	each
i	í	of
i	í	to
íþróttamaðr	íþróttamaður	sports-man
jafnstórliga	jafnstórlega	equally-great
kallaðr	kallaður	called
kallat	kallað	called
kemr	kemur	come
kenna	kenn	know
kjörit	kjörið	choice
kœmi	kæmu	came

A Word Comparison of Old Norse and Old Icelandic

Old Norse	Old Icelandic	English	Old Norse	Old Icelandic	English
komit	komið	comes	mik	mig	me
komit	komið	coming	mikit	mikið	many
kostr	kostur	choice	missmíði	missmíð	mistake
lætr	lætur	behaviour	mjök	mjög	much
látim	látum	let	mögr	mögur	skinny
leggr	leggur	lay	munngát	mungát	ale
leið	á	the	muntú	muntu	should
leita	leiða	objection	munu	munuð	shall
leitat	leitað	sought	næða	næði	neared
léttra	lettara	easier	nafnfrægr	nafndrægur	named
lézt	lést	burden	nefndr	nefndur	named
lézt	lést	let	neitaða	neitaði	refusal
liðveizlunni	liðveilsunni	supportive	neitaða	neitaði	refused
limit	limið	foliage	niðrfall	niðurfall	dropping
litill	lítill	little	nökkura	nokkura	some
Litill	lítill	small	nökkurar	nokkurar	some
litilræði	lítilræði	little-advised	nökkurir	nokkurir	some
lízt	líst	beholding	nökkurn	nokkurn	someone
lízt	líst	like	nökkuru	nokkuru	somewhat
ljótr	ljótur	ugly	nökkut	nokkuð	some
lög-(sögu)maðr	lögmaður	law-speaker	nökkut	nokkuð	something
lokit	lokið	ended	norðr	norðu	north
Länguhlið	länguhlíð	Langahlid (place)	norðr	norður	north
			nóttina	nótt	night
lúkim	lúkum	conclude	Œrr	ær	awed
lýkr	lýkur	ends	ofarliga	ofarlega	high-up
lýsír	lýsir	declared	ofreflismenn	ofureflismenn	ultra-strong-men
maðr	maður	a-man			
maðr	maður	man	oftliga	oftlega	often
mælti	mætli	said	óhœfan	óhæfan	trouble
mælti	mætli	spoke	ok	og	also
mælti	segir	said	ok	og	and
mágr	mágur	brother-in-law	okkarr	okkar	ours
málit	málið	matter	okkr	okkur	ours
málit	málið	the-matter	okkr	okkur	us
málkunnigr	málkunnigur	talking-known	Ólíkligt	ólíklegt	unlike
manna	mann	men	ómakligr	ómaklegur	uncomfortable
manna	mönnum	men	ópit	ópið	open
mannamunr	mannamunur	integrity	ór	úr	from
margt	mart	many	ór	úr	of
mega	megi	may	ór	úr	out-of
mér	þér	you	orðit	orðið	word

90

A Word Comparison of Old Norse and Old Icelandic

Old Norse	Old Icelandic	English
órhjarta	örhjarta	un-heartened
Ormr	ormur	orm
óvizku	ósvisku	unwise
ráðit	ráðið	decided
ráttlátir	réttlátir	right-like
reið	fór	travelled
reitt	reiðst	riding
reitt	reiðst	rode
riða	ríða	ride
riða	ríða	rode
rœddu	ræddu	discussed
sá	sáu	this
sáttu	sástu	saw-you
sé	muni	should
sem	ssem	as
sérhverjum	sér	theirs
siðan	síðan	then
siðr	siður	custom
sjálfdœmi	sjálfdæmi	self-judgement
sjálfr	sjálfur	himself
sjúkr	sínkur	stingy
skaltú	skaltu	shall-you
skarðit	skarð	gap
skarðit	skarðið	the-pass
skerða	skríða	action
skifta	skipta	exchange
Skildist	skildust	separated
skilit	skilið	divided
skilit	skilið	understood
skógana	skóga	forest
skóggangssök	skóggang	outlawry
Skógr	skógur	forest
Skulu	skuluð	should
skylda	skyldi	should
skyldi	skyldu	should
skyldim	skyldum	should
skylim	skulum	should
Slikt	slíkt	such
slöðraði	slauðraði	trailing-behind
snýr	snýrð	turned
sœmd	sæmd	honour
sœmdunum	sæmdunum	honour
Sökunautr	sökunautur	defendant
stalt	stalst	stealing
stefnda	stefndi	summonsed
Steingrimr	steingrímur	Steingrim (name)
stikat	stikað	stitched
stórorðr	stórorðu	high-sounding
stungizt	stungist	wounded
sumarit	sumarið	summer
sundr	sundur	asunder
svá	sogört	saying
svá	svo	so
svá	svo	such
svarar	segir	said
svarar	svaraði	answered
Svíðingi	sviðningi	Svidning (place)
synjat	synjað	refused
talaða	talaði	said
þá	sá	so
þá	þú	you
þakksamliga	þakksamlega	thankfully
þar	það	that
þat	það	it
þat	það	that
þat	það	the
þat	það	this
þat	það	to
þat	það	with
þat	þess	this
Þörðarson	þórðarson	Thordarson (name)
Þörkels	þorkels	Thorkell (name)
þeira	þeim	these
þeira	þeirra	of-the
þeira	þeirra	their
þeira	þeirra	theirs
þeira	þeirra	them
þeira	þeirra	they
þeira	þeirra	those
þér	það	that

A Word Comparison of Old Norse and Old Icelandic

Old Norse	Old Icelandic	English
þess	þessa	this
þessa	þá	then
þik	þig	you
þingit	þingið	assembly
þit	þið	you
þó	þá	then
þó	þótt	though
þœtti	þótti	thought
Þórhallr	þórhalldur	Thorhall (name)
Þórhallr	þórhallur	Thorhall (name)
Þórkel	þorkel	Thorkell (name)
Þórkeli	þorkeli	Thorkell (name)
Þórkell	þorkell	Thorkell (name)
Þórkels	þorkels	Thorkell (name)
Þórstein	þorstein	Thorstein (name)
Þórsteinn	þorsteinn	Thorstein (name)
Þórsteins	þorsteins	Thorstein (name)
Þórsteins	þorsteins	Thorstein's (name)
þótt	þót	though
þriði	þriðji	third
Þurfu	þurfa	need
Því	hví	why
því	það	that
Þykki	þykir	think
þykkir	þykir	seems
þykkjast	þykjast	consider
til	itl	little
tiltœkilegt	tiltækilegra	available
tœki	tæki	took
tvá	tvo	two
váðaverk	voðaverk	accidents
væra	væri	would-be
væri	væru	were
væri	var	was
ván	von	hope
ván	von	wished
Vápnafjörð	vopnafjörð	Vopnafjord (place)
vár	vor	spring
vár	voru	are
Varðtú	varðstu	were-you
varit	varið	defend
várkunn	vorkunn	pity
várr	vor	our
várra	vorra	talking-loudly
vart	varst	were
várþings	vorþings	local-assembly
váru	voru	was
váru	voru	were
varut	voruð	were
vátta	votta	witness
váttar	vottar	witnesses
váttnefna	vottnefna	witnesses
vegr	vegur	way
veitit	veitið	know
Veittú	veittu	grant
vér	við	on
vér	við	we
verðr	verður	worth
verit	verið	been
vestr	vestur	west
vetrinn	veturinn	winter
vilda	vildi	willed
vili	vilji	willing
vilit	viljið	will
vilnat	vilnað	willed
vindr	vindur	wind
víss	vís	aware
vit	vér	we
vit	við	we
vit	við	with
vitu	vita	knowing
yðr	yður	yours
ykkr	ykkur	you
yrði	yrðu	be

www.ingramcontent.com/pod-product-compliance
Lightning Source LLC
Chambersburg PA
CBHW051420070526
44584CB00023B/3517